First International Workshop on Digital Disease Detection Using Social Media (DDDSM 2017)

Taipei, Taiwan
27 November 2017

ISBN: 978-1-5108-5299-0

Printed from e-media with permission by:

Curran Associates, Inc.
57 Morehouse Lane
Red Hook, NY 12571

Some format issues inherent in the e-media version may also appear in this print version.

Printed by Curran Associates, Inc. (2017)

For permission requests, please contact the Association for Computational Linguistics at the address below.

Association for Computational Linguistics
209 N. Eighth Street
Stroudsburg, Pennsylvania 18360

Phone: 1-570-476-8006
Fax: 1-570-476-0860

acl@aclweb.org

Additional copies of this publication are available from:

Curran Associates, Inc.
57 Morehouse Lane
Red Hook, NY 12571 USA
Phone: 845-758-0400
Fax: 845-758-2633
Email: curran@proceedings.com
Web: www.proceedings.com

DDDSM 2017

The First International Workshop on Digital Disease Detection using Social Media

Proceedings of the Workshop

November 27, 2017
Taipei, Taiwan

Gold Sponsor

Australian National Health and Medical Research Council's (NHMRC) Centre for Research Excellence in Integrated System for Epidemic Surveillance (ISER)

Silver Sponsor

World Health Organization(WHO) Collaborating Centre for eHealth (AUS-92)

Bronze Sponsor

iq-t.com

Introduction

Welcome to the first international Workshop on Digital Disease Detection using Social Media 2017 (DDDSM-2017) http://www.dddsm.org/, co-located with the The 8th International Joint Conference on Natural Language Processing (IJCNLP 2017).

Historically, disease outbreaks such as Ebola and Zika outbreaks were detected based on trends observed in the official reports collected at various geographic levels, as part of the pre-established disease surveillance programs. The major drawback of this approach is producing outbreak alerts in timely fashion. Advances in technology and rapid adoption of information sharing platforms such as social media platforms provide new data sources and unique opportunities for researchers to investigate disease outbreaks. Digital disease detection involves monitoring various digital information sources for early warning, detection, rapid response, and management phases of surveillance. Unlike manual systems, which relies on traditional disease surveillance program reports to monitor and predict early outbreaks, the current automated digital disease surveillance systems exploit mainly publicly available information on internet such as social media, news and search engine data.

The DDDSM workshop emphasizes the application of the latest advances in natural language processing on social media data to detect early outbreak signals. In addition, the goals of this workshop are i) to disseminate the scientific knowledge in the area of outbreak detection using social media data; ii) make the NLP community aware of the disease outbreak detection aspects and iii) exchange ideas, challenges and experiences in using social media data for disease surveillance purposes.

The workshop has received submissions covering topics: vaccination sentiment , syndromic surveillance for mental health, Gastroenteritis and flu and identification of pregnant women on social media, and digital disease detection competitions. Each submission has been peer-reviewed by 3 members from the program committee with at least one member with background and training in public health. The accepted papers are into two sessions as oral presentations. It is our pleasure to bring together researchers from Public Health, Natural Language Processing and Data science disciplines under one-roof for this one-day workshop.

We would like to acknowledge the program committee for their meticulous work, without whom this workshop might not have been possible. We also would like to thank the authors for considering to submit their work to DDDSM 2017 workshop. We personally would like to thank the IJCNLP 2017 organisers to host the DDDSM workshop.

Funding for this workshop is provided by School of Public Health and Community Medicine, UNSW Sydney. https://sphcm.med.unsw.edu.au/. We also would like to thank the ISER, WHO Collaborating centre for eHealth and IQ-Technology for their generous sponsorship.

We sincerely hope that the participants of this workshop take home some interesting research ideas, projects and , most importantly new friendships and collaborations. We wish you all a productive workshop and safe journey, back home.

- Jitendra Jonnagaddala, Hong-Jie Dai and Yung-Chun Chang

Organizers:

Jitendra Jonnagaddala, School of Public Health and Community Medicine, UNSW Sydney, Australia
Hong-Jie Dai, Department of Computer Science and Information Engineering, National Taitung University, Taiwan
Yung-Chun Chang, Graduate Institute of Data Science, Taipei Medical University, Taiwan

Program Committee:

Siaw-Teng Liaw, UNSW Sydney , Australia
Abrar Chughtai, UNSW Sydney, Australia
Dillon Adam, UNSW Sydney, Australia
Chau Bui, UNSW Sydney, Australia
Padmanesan Narasimhan, UNSW Sydney, Australia
Mahfuz Ashraf, UNSW Sydney, Australia
Chih-Hao Ku - Lawrence Technological University, USA
Swapna Gottipati, Singapore Management University
Feiyan Hu, Dublin City University
Karin Verspoor, The University of Melbourne, Australia
Dingcheng Li, Research scientist Baidu, USA
Lun-Wei Ku, Academia Sinica, Taiwan
Jheng-Long Wu, Academia Sinica, Taiwan
Nai-Wen Chang, Academia Sinica, Taiwan
Yu-Lun Hsieh - Academia Sinica, Taiwan
Chien Chin Chen, National Taiwan University, Taiwan
Hen-Hsen Huang, National Taiwan University, Taiwan
I-Jen Chiang, Taipei Medical University, Taiwan
Hui-Chun Hung, Taipei Medical University, Taiwan
Emily Chia-Yu Su, Taipei Medical University, Taiwan
Richard Tzong-Han Tsai, National Central University, Taiwan
Min-Yuh Day, Tamkang University, Taiwan

Table of Contents

Automatic detection of stance towards vaccination in online discussion forums
Maria Skeppstedt, Andreas Kerren and Manfred Stede 1

Analysing the Causes of Depressed Mood from Depression Vulnerable Individuals
Noor Fazilla Abd Yusof, Chenghua Lin and Frank Guerin 9

Multivariate Linear Regression of Symptoms-related Tweets for Infectious Gastroenteritis Scale Estimation
Ryo Takeuchi, Hayate ISO, Kaoru Ito, Shoko Wakamiya and Eiji Aramaki 18

Incorporating Dependency Trees Improve Identification of Pregnant Women on Social Media Platforms
Yi-Jie Huang, Chu Hsien Su, Yi-Chun Chang, Tseng-Hsin Ting, Tzu-Yuan Fu, Rou-Min Wang, Hong-Jie Dai, Yung-Chun Chang, Jitendra Jonnagaddala and Wen-Lian Hsu 26

Using a Recurrent Neural Network Model for Classification of Tweets Conveyed Influenza-related Information
Chen-Kai Wang, Onkar Singh, Zhao-Li Tang and Hong-Jie Dai 33

ZikaHack 2016: A digital disease detection competition
Dillon C Adam, Jitendra Jonnagaddala, Daniel Han-Chen, Sean Batongbacal, Luan Almeida, Jing Z Zhu, Jenny J Yang, Jumail M Mundekkat, Steven Badman, Abrar Chughtai and C Raina MacIntyre 39

A Method to Generate a Machine-Labeled Data for Biomedical Named Entity Recognition with Various Sub-Domains
Juae Kim, Sunjae Kwon, Youngjoong Ko and Jungyun Seo 47

Enhancing Drug-Drug Interaction Classification with Corpus-level Feature and Classifier Ensemble
Jing Cyun Tu, Po-Ting Lai and Richard Tzong-Han Tsai 52

Chemical-Induced Disease Detection Using Invariance-based Pattern Learning Model
Neha Warikoo, Yung-Chun Chang and Wen-Lian Hsu 57

Conference Program

Monday, November 27, 2017

08:30–09:00 *Opening remarks*
Jitendra Jonnagaddala

09:00–12:00 Morning Session: Oral Presentations

09:00–09:30 *Automatic detection of stance towards vaccination in online discussion forums*
Maria Skeppstedt, Andreas Kerren and Manfred Stede

09:30–10:00 *Analysing the Causes of Depressed Mood from Depression Vulnerable Individuals*
Noor Fazilla Abd Yusof, Chenghua Lin and Frank Guerin

10:00–10:30 *Multivariate Linear Regression of Symptoms-related Tweets for Infectious Gastroenteritis Scale Estimation*
Ryo Takeuchi, Hayate ISO, Kaoru Ito, Shoko Wakamiya and Eiji Aramaki

10:30–11:00 *Break*

11:00–11:30 *Incorporating Dependency Trees Improve Identification of Pregnant Women on Social Media Platforms*
Yi-Jie Huang, Chu Hsien Su, Yi-Chun Chang, Tseng-Hsin Ting, Tzu-Yuan Fu, Rou-Min Wang, Hong-Jie Dai, Yung-Chun Chang, Jitendra Jonnagaddala and Wen-Lian Hsu

11:30–12:00 *Using a Recurrent Neural Network Model for Classification of Tweets Conveyed Influenza-related Information*
Chen-Kai Wang, Onkar Singh, Zhao-Li Tang and Hong-Jie Dai

12:00–13:30 *Lunch*

Monday, November 27, 2017 (continued)

13:30–16:15 Afternoon Session: Mini-Oral Presentations

13:30–13:50 *ZikaHack 2016: A digital disease detection competition*
Dillon C Adam, Jitendra Jonnagaddala, Daniel Han-Chen, Sean Batongbacal, Luan Almeida, Jing Z Zhu, Jenny J Yang, Jumail M Mundekkat, Steven Badman, Abrar Chughtai and C Raina MacIntyre

13:50–14:10 *A Method to Generate a Machine-Labeled Data for Biomedical Named Entity Recognition with Various Sub-Domains*
Juae Kim, Sunjae Kwon, Youngjoong Ko and Jungyun Seo

14:10–14:30 *Enhancing Drug-Drug Interaction Classification with Corpus-level Feature and Classifier Ensemble*
Jing Cyun Tu, Po-Ting Lai and Richard Tzong-Han Tsai

14:30–14:50 *Chemical-Induced Disease Detection Using Invariance-based Pattern Learning Model*
Neha Warikoo, Yung-Chun Chang and Wen-Lian Hsu

14:50–15:30 ***Break***

15:30–16:00 *Open Discussion*
Chairs: Jitendra Jonnagaddala, Yung-Chun Chang and Hong-Jie Dai

16:00–16:15 *Closing remarks*
Jitendra Jonnagaddala

Automatic detection of stance towards vaccination in online discussion forums

Maria Skeppstedt[1,2], **Andreas Kerren**[1], **Manfred Stede**[2]
[1]Computer Science Department, Linnaeus University, Växjö, Sweden
{maria.skeppstedt,andreas.kerren}@lnu.se
[2]Applied Computational Linguistics, University of Potsdam, Potsdam, Germany
stede@uni-potsdam.de

Abstract

A classifier for automatic detection of stance towards vaccination in online forums was trained and evaluated. Debate posts from six discussion threads on the British parental website Mumsnet were manually annotated for stance *against* or *for* vaccination, or as *undecided*. A support vector machine, trained to detect the three classes, achieved a macro F-score of 0.44, while a macro F-score of 0.62 was obtained by the same type of classifier on the binary classification task of distinguishing stance *against* vaccination from stance *for* vaccination. These results show that vaccine stance detection in online forums is a difficult task, at least for the type of model investigated and for the relatively small training corpus that was used. Future work will therefore include an expansion of the training data and an evaluation of other types of classifiers and features.

1 Introduction

There have been outbreaks of vaccine-preventable diseases that were caused by decreased vaccination rates, which in turn were due to negative attitudes towards vaccination. Two examples are an outbreak of polio in 2003-2004, which started in northern Nigeria and spread to 15 other countries (Larson and Ghinai, 2011), and an outbreak of measles in Minnesota in 2017 (Modarressy-Tehrani, 2017).

Information on vaccination can be gathered from many different types of sources. A survey among British parents showed that 34% consulted web-based resources for vaccination information (Campbell et al., 2017). The survey also showed that 31% of the parents that had consulted chat rooms or discussion forums had seen information that "would make them doubt having their child(ren) immunised or persuade them not to immunise", compared to 23% for parents consulting Twitter and 8% among all parents included in the survey.

Discussion forums thus form an important outlet for vaccine hesitancy, and this genre might therefore be relevant to automatically monitor for an increase in posts that express a negative stance towards vaccination. Most previous work on training and evaluation of classifiers for automatic detection of vaccination stance has, however, been carried out on tweets. In this study, we therefore take on the task of automatic vaccine stance detection of debate posts in online discussion forums.

2 Background

Mohammad et al. (2017) define *stance detection* as "[...] the task of automatically determining from text whether the author of the text is in favor of, against, or neutral toward a proposition or target". They distinguish stance detection from the better known task of sentiment analysis by that "in stance detection, systems are to determine favorability toward a given (pre-chosen) target of in terest", whereas sentiment analysis is the task of "determining whether a piece of text is positive, negative, or neutral, or determining from text the speakers opinion and the target of the opinion". For instance, the utterance "The diseases that vaccination can protect you from are horrible" expresses a stance *for* the pre-chosen target "vaccination", while expressing a *negative* sentiment towards the sentiment-target "diseases".

This definition of stance is used in several stance detection studies. For instance, in studies performed on the text genres web debate forums (Somasundaran and Wiebe, 2010; Anand et al.,

Proceedings of the International Workshop on Digital Disease Detection using Social Media 2017 (DDDSM-2017), pages 1–8,
Taipei, Taiwan, November 27, 2017.

2011; Walker et al., 2012; Hasan and Ng, 2013), news paper text (Ferreira and Vlachos, 2016; Fake News Challenge, 2017) and tweets (Augenstein et al., 2016; Mohammad et al., 2017).

Stance detection is generally considered more difficult than sentiment analysis and thereby a task for which currently available methods achieve lower results. This was, for instance, shown by a recent shared task on three-category stance classification of tweets, where an F-score of 0.59 was achieved by a classifier that outperformed submissions from 19 shared task teams (Mohammad et al., 2017). For the task of stance classification of posts of two-sided discussion threads, an F-score of 0.70 is the best result we have been able to find in previous research (Hasan and Ng, 2013)[1].

Previous studies on attitudes towards vaccination do not make use of the term stance, but discuss negative/positive sentiment towards vaccination. There are a number of such sentiment detection studies conducted on tweets, while studies on online forums, to the best of our knowledge, are limited to the task of topic modelling (Tangherlini et al., 2016).

Most vaccination sentiment studies have been conducted on tweets that contain keywords related to HPV (human papillomavirus) vaccination. In one of these, 1,470 HPV-related tweets were manually categorised according to sentiment towards the HPV vaccine (positive, negative, neutral, or no mention). A decision tree was thereafter trained to perform the sentiment classification, and a leave-one-out evaluation resulted in an AUC score of 0.92 (Massey et al., 2016). Another HPV study applied a three-level hierarchical classification scheme and 6,000 tweets were manually categorised as (i) related or unrelated to HPV vaccination, (ii) positive, negative or neutral towards vaccination and (iii) whether they concerned safety, efficacy, emotional resistance, cost and others (Du et al., 2017). A hierarchical classification scheme corresponding to the hierarchy of the categories was applied in the form of support vector machine classifiers, which resulted in a micro-average F-score of 0.74 and a macro-average F-score of 0.59. In a third HPV study, tweets were annotated into the binary category of whether they expressed an anti-vaccine opinion or not (1,050 tweets as training data and 1,100 as test data). A support vector machine trained on bigrams achieved an F-score of 0.82 for detecting negative tweets.

Tweets on the A(H1N1) influenza vaccine have also been automatically classified (Salathé and Khandelwal, 2011). 47,143 tweets that contained keywords related to vaccination were manually classified into four categories; positive/negative/neutral sentiment towards vaccination, or not concerning the A(H1N1) vaccine. The 630 tweets that had been classified by at least 44 annotators, and for which more than 50% of these annotators had selected the same category were used as evaluation data. The rest of the annotated data was used for training a machine learning model in the form of an ensemble classifier built on a Naive Bayes and a Maximum Entropy classifier. This resulted in a classifier accuracy of 0.84.

There are also a number of studies in which purely manual analyses of opinions on vaccination have been carried out. For instance, analyses of blog posts (Brien et al., 2013), online forums (Skea et al., 2008), and of reports on vaccination in many different types of online materials (Larson et al., 2013). Data from the latter analysis has been incorporated into a disease surveillance tool and used for comparing sentiment towards vaccination in different parts of North America (Powell et al., 2016b). However, as pointed out by Powell et al. (2016a), to be able to use this kind of surveillance tool for vaccine-preventable diseases on a larger scale, manual analyses are not enough. Instead, the functionality that we investigate here is required, that is to be able to automatically detect stance towards vaccination. While previous studies on detection of stance/sentiment towards specific types of vaccines in tweets have have been carried out, we here aim to investigate the possibility of automatic vaccine stance detection in the important genre of online discussion forums.

3 Method

A corpus was first compiled and pre-processed, and thereafter annotated for stance towards vaccination. The annotated corpus was then used to train models to detect the stance categories.[2]

[1] For these two studies, F-score refers to macro F-score calculated over five and four different stance targets, respectively. This figure was not reported in the paper by Hasan and Ng (2013), but was calculated here from the best results reported for each target. From experiments by Hasan and Ng (2013) that included non-textual features and information from other posts from the same debater, better results than these have been reported.

[2] The code used for the experiments, as well as the annotation and post meta-data (Mumsnet ID, debater, debate thread)

3.1 Corpus selection

The experiment was carried out on discussion threads from the British parental website Mumsnet, which is a site that hosts online forums where users discuss and share information on parenting and other topics.[3] We based the choice of forum on the reasoning provided by Skea et al. (2008). They chose Mumsnet for manual analysis of vaccine stance, as the site contains discussion threads on many different topics and therefore is likely to attract a more diverse set of debaters than e.g., an anti-vaccination site. In addition, the discussion threads are publicly available without a login and the debaters are asked to anonymise their postings, e.g., by using a chat nickname. This makes it less likely that the posts include content that debaters would like to keep private.

Mumsnet lists a large number of main discussion topics, of which vaccination is one. The debaters can either choose a main topic and start a new discussion thread on a more specific topic, e.g., "Refusing to vaccinate your child", or submit a post to an existing thread. We extracted posts from the six discussion threads, which, given their name, we assessed as most likely to spur a debate *against/for* vaccination. The topics of all threads with more than 80 posts and for which the latest post was written between the years 2011 and 2017 were considered (68 threads). Only thread names that encouraged discussions on child vaccination in general were included, while debates on more specific aspects on vaccination or vaccination for specific diseases were excluded. Examples of topics excluded for these reasons were "Vaccinations and nursery schools", "Staggering Vaccinations?" or "HPV gardasil[4]". Other types of threads excluded were those with a yes/no question as thread name, as answers to these might be more difficult to understand without context, and threads asking for explanations for an opposite view — e.g., "Please explain, succinctly, the anti vac argument." — as such threads might prompt debaters to list opinions of opponents rather than to express their own arguments.

3.2 Corpus pre-processing and filtering

The text and meta-data of the discussion posts could be extracted from the html-pages based on their *div class*. Html tags in the text were removed and the text was segmented into paragraphs using jusText (Pomikálek, 2011).

Texts previously written by other debaters are sometimes copied into new posts in order to indicate that a comment to this previous post is made (the posts are all posted on the same level, and there is no functionality for posting an answer to a specific previous post). Although the debaters do not use a uniform approach to indicate that text has been copied from another debater, we devised a simple method for removing as many instances as possible of copied text. Paragraphs that were exclusively constructed of sentences that had occurred in previous posts were removed, using the standard sentence segmentation included in NLTK (Natural Language Toolkit) for sentence matching (Bird, 2002). In addition, text chunks longer than three words that were marked in bold or by double quotation were removed, in order to exclude citations in general, from other debaters as well as from external sources. Also names of opponents are sometimes mentioned in the posts, as a means to indicate that the content of the post is addressed to a specific opponent debater. These names were also automatically removed.

Similar to previous vaccination studies on tweets, we considered the content of each debate post without the context of surrounding posts. To increase the likelihood that the debater's stance towards vaccination would be interpretable without context, only posts containing at least one of the following character combinations were included in the experiment: *vacc / vax / jab / immunis / immuniz*. The removal of posts that did not contain these character combinations resulted in that the original set of 2,225 debate posts included in the six extracted threads was reduced to a set of 1,190 posts. These 1,190 posts (written by 136 different authors) were manually annotated and used in the machine learning experiment.

3.3 Annotation

The 1,190 posts to include in the experiment were presented for manual classification in a random order, without revealing who the debater was or which thread the post belonged to. The annotation was performed by one of the authors of the paper.

Following the principle of the guidelines by Mohammad et al. (2017), we classified the posts as taking a stance *against* or *for* vaccination, or

is available at: `github.com/mariask2/vaccination_stance`

[3] `www.mumsnet.com/Talk`

[4] The name of a vaccine.

to be *undecided*. The third category was applied to posts in which the debater explicitly declared to be undecided, as well as to posts for which the debater's stance towards vaccination could not be determined. The post did not have to explicitly support or oppose vaccination to be classified according to the categories *against* or *for*, but it was enough if an opposition or support could be inferred from the post. The stance taken could, for instance, be conveyed without actually mentioning vaccination, as in "You are very lucky to live in the west, and you are free to make that decision because the majority are giving you herd immunity." It could also be conveyed through an agreement or disagreement with a known proponent/opponent of vaccination, as the statement "Andrew Wakefield is a proven liar and a profiteer — therefore his "research" is irrelevant to any sane, rational discussion [...]" Web links to external resources were, however, not included in the classification decision, even when a stance towards vaccination could be inferred from the name of the URL.

Mohammad et al. (2017) did not specify in detail how to distinguish between stance *against* and *for* the targets included in the study. However, several of the posts in our data did not express a clear positive or clear negative stance towards vaccination in general, and we therefore needed more detailed guidelines for how to draw the line between *against* and *for*. We adopted the basic rule of classifying the post as *against* vaccination when the debater expressed a stance that opposed an official vaccination policy, e.g., as recommended in the health care system. This included, for instance, posts that expressed criticism against some of the recommended vaccines but an acceptance of others, or an acceptance of vaccination in general but not of the officially recommended vaccination scheme. The post "I challenge my DD vaccine schedule all the time. Last time I refused to allow her have MMR with yet another vaccine just because a government quango says so [...]" was thereby classified as *against* vaccination, although the debater is not negative towards all forms of vaccination. Posts that contained a concern over waning immunity from vaccination were classified as *undecided*, except when this concern was used as an argument against vaccination. Posts that expressed a stance against compulsory vaccination, without revealing a stance on vaccination in general, were also classified as *undecided*.

3.4 Machine learning experiments

A standard text classification approach, in the form of a linear support vector machine model, was applied to the task of automatically classifying the debate posts. This follows the approach of Mohammad et al. (2017), as well as of many of the previously performed vaccine sentiment studies. The model was trained on all tokens in the training data, as well as on 2-, 3- and 4-grams that occurred at least twice in the data. The standard NLTK stop word list for English was used for removing non-content words when constructing one set of n-grams. An additional set of n-grams was generated with a reduced version of this stop word list, which mainly consisted of articles, forms of copula, and forms of "it", "have" and "do". The reason for using a reduced list was that negations, pronouns etc. that were included in the standard NLTK stop word list can be important cues for classifying argumentative text.

Two types of classifiers were trained: one to perform the task of classifying posts into all three categories annotated, and the other one to perform the task of distinguishing posts annotated as *against* vaccination from those annotated as *for* vaccination. The classifiers were implemented using scikit-learn's LinearSVC class with the default settings. For training/evaluation, we applied cross-validation on the 1,190 annotated posts. Due to the relatively small data size, we used 30 folds, instead of the more standard approach of 10 folds.

4 Results

Average F-scores for the classifiers and the confusion matrix was calculated using the standard functionality in scikit-learn[5]. Macro average F-scores of 0.44 and 0.62 were achieved for the three-class classifier and for the binary classifier, respectively (Table 1). The confusion matrix and the precision/recall scores for the three-class classifier show that there were frequent misclassifications between all three categories (Table 2). It can also be derived from this table that there was an even distribution between posts annotated as taking a stance *against* vaccination (41%) and those taking a stance *for* vaccination (38%).

[5] sklearn.metrics.f1_score

Classifier	Micro	Macro
against / for / undecided	0.48	0.44
against / for	0.62	0.62

Table 1: Macro and micro F-score for the two experiments, i.e., (i) a classifier that classifies posts as taking a stance *against* and *for* vaccination or being *undecided* and (ii) a binary classifier that classifies posts as *against* or *for* vaccination.

		Classified as:			
		against	*for*	*undec.*	total
Anno-tated as:	*against*	275	148	70	493
	for	137	240	73	450
	undec.	101	89	57	247
		against	*for*	*undec.*	
	Precision	0.54	0.53	0.29	
	Recall	0.56	0.50	0.23	

Table 2: Confusion matrix and precision/recall-scores for the three-class classifier. The table also shows the total number of posts annotated as *against*, *for* or *undecided*.

5 Discussion

Similar to what as been shown in previous stance detection studies, the detection of stance towards vaccination was proven to be a difficult task, at least for the type of model investigated and for the relatively small training corpus used. Results cannot be directly compared to previous studies, as there are a number factors that vary between the studies. For instance, the number of training samples used, evaluation measures applied, as well as criteria in some previous studies for excluding samples from the data set that were difficult to classify. There is, however, a large difference between the results achieved here, and some of the previous studies on detection of sentiment towards vaccination, which probably cannot be accounted for by these variations. Instead, it is likely that these differences are due to that the previous studies i) were conducted on tweets, and ii) used a more precise stance target. As tweets are short, they are likely to be more to the point than the more elaborate and longer discussions of the debate forums that we used, and therefore easier for stance detection. The more precise stance target is likely to result in that a more limited set of topics are discussed, which are easier to learn compared to the more wide stance target of vaccination in general that we applied. In future work, the training corpus will be expanded in order to explore if this can improve results. In addition, an evaluation of a wider range of machine learning methods and features will be conducted.

For constructing the corpus used here, a number of decisions had to be made. In the following sections we reflect on these decisions and make a number of suggestions for future studies.

5.1 Annotation decisions

The decision to treat each debate post as one independent unit without taking its context into account is not self-evident, as a post is more meaningful to interpret in the context of its discussion thread. Taking the context into account for determining the stance would, however, also entail a more complex classification task. At least in a first step in future work, we will therefore concentrate on the types of debate posts that can be interpreted without context. Research on online forums by Anand et al. (2011) has shown that the incorporation of features from the previous post can improve the performance of a stance classifier for posts that express rebuttals. This work, however, used meta-data of the debaters' stance for training the classifiers and did not provide the option to classify a post as undecided when its stance could not be determined without its debate context.

Another possible approach to take would be to classify *debaters* according to the stance they take, instead of classifying each individual post into a stance. The set of debate posts written by one debater would then be treated as one unit of text, and the assumption that debaters do not change their stance within a discussion thread would have to be made. Previous research has shown that stance classification of posts in online forums can be improved by also taking classifier output from other posts by the same author into account (Hasan and Ng, 2013).

On the same assumption that debaters do not change their stance, it might also be possible to give some kind of measure of the validity of the stance annotations. If the annotations are to be considered valid, posts from the same debater should ideally always take the same stance, or at least only exceptionally take the opposite stance. Such a measure could be used as a complement to annotator agreement that measures reliability rather than validity (Artstein and Poesio, 2008). Annotator agreement should, however, also be measured.

Previous studies on stance do not reason to a

large extent on where to draw the line between the categories *against* and *for* the target. In the case of previous vaccination stance studies, this might be explained by that these studies have focused on attitudes towards one specific type of vaccine; whereas stance towards vaccination in general is a larger issue with a wider range of possible nuances among debaters' opinions. Mohammad et al. (2017), on the other hand, used broader targets, e.g., "Feminist movement" and "Atheism", but left the task of drawing the line between *against* and *for* to the annotators. Eight annotators classified each tweet, and only the subset of tweets for which at least 60% of the annotators agreed on the classification were retained in the data set.

Other studies have circumvented the problem of giving an exact definition of stance towards a target by using data sets from debate portals, where meta-data on the debaters' stance is provided. Our decision, to classify debate posts as *against* vaccination when they opposed an official vaccination policy, was based on that debaters often implicitly argue against such a policy. In addition, a system for surveilling increases in vaccine hesitancy is likely to take an official policy as its point of departure.

The eight annotators that classified each tweet in the study by Mohammad et al. (2017) were employed through a crowdsourcing platform, which was made possible by that the stance targets were chosen with the criterion that they should be commonly known in the United States. For annotating stance on vaccination, however, annotators with some amount of prior knowledge of vaccine debate topics and vaccine controversies might be preferred. Crowdsourcing might therefore not be a viable option for this annotation task.

40 randomly selected posts that did not fulfil the criterion of containing any of the selected vaccine-related filter terms, and which therefore had been excluded from the study, were also annotated. Although this set is too small to make any definite conclusions, the relatively large proportion of posts in the set that expressed a stance *against* or *for* vaccination (25%) indicates that the filtering criterion used was too crude and led to the exclusion of relevant posts. Future studies should therefore either apply a better filtering criterion, or include all discussion thread posts in an annotation and machine learning study.

5.2 Machine learning decisions

The choice of machine learning model was primarily based on that a linear support vector machine was successful on data from the previously mentioned shared task of stance detection of tweets (Mohammad et al., 2017). This model outperformed submissions from teams that used methods which might intuitively be better adapted to the task, i.e., an LSTM classifier (Augenstein et al., 2016). Support vector machines have also been used in many of the previous vaccine sentiment studies. In addition, a linear support vector machine classifier is also a standard method that is often used for different types of text classification tasks (Manning et al., 2008, pp. 335-337). The model is for these reasons suitable to use as a baseline against which to compare future experiments on the vaccine stance classification task.

Despite being the most successful method for stance detection of tweets, it is likely that a support vector machine, trained on word and character n-grams in the entire text is not the optimal method for stance detection of discussion posts. First of all, discussion thread posts are typically longer than a tweet and consist of several sentences, which often each of them form an own argument with a relatively independent content. A classifier that operates on the level of a sentence, or other shorter parts of the text, and combines the stance classification of each of these segments into a post-level classification might be better suited to the task. For instance, Hasan and Ng (2013) improved their stance classification results by expanding their feature set to also include an unsupervised estimation of the stance of each sentence in the debate post.

In addition, it is likely that even if applied on a sentence-level, the use of n-grams would not capture the full complexity of the argumentative text genre. Instead, the structure of the words in the sentences might need to be incorporated in the feature set. A classifier trained on a token-level and where neighbouring tokens in a large context window are incorporated as features could be one such approach. Another possibility would be the previously mentioned approach of stance detection using an LSTM classifier (Augenstein et al., 2016).

Previous studies have also been able to improve results, at least for some targets, by incorporating other features than n-grams. For instance, features constructed using an arguing lexicon (Somasundaran and Wiebe, 2010), or word embeddings constructed in an unsupervised fashion using a large corpus from the same text genre as the text to classify (Mohammad et al., 2017).

Apart from making a decision on what type of classifier and features to use, it must also be decided on how to gather more training data. Strategies for reducing the manual labelling effort should be investigated, in particular since the annotation task, as discussed above, might not be suitable for crowdsourcing. One possible approach would be to use weakly supervised data. Posts from vaccine-related discussion threads contrasted with posts from other discussion threads might be used as weakly supervised data for classifying posts as either taking a stance on vaccination or being undecided. Weakly supervised data for classifying into stance *against* or *for* vaccination could be gathered by using the assumption that debaters do not change their stance within a thread. A few posts from each of the debaters would then be manually annotated and the rest of the posts from this debater would automatically be assigned the same stance category. Hasan and Ng (2013) improved results by incorporating weakly labelled data that was gathered through harvesting text adjacent to phrases that, with a large confidence, are indicators of stance *against* or *for* the target in question.

It can be noted that the number of contributors to each discussion thread seems to be rather small, as the posts annotated for the experiment had been written by only 136 debaters. Future experiments on this data set and its extensions should therefore evaluate to what extent a classifier trained on the Mumsnet data is able to detect vaccination stance in discussion threads in general. That is, to make sure the models have avoided overfitting on the language typical to a small set of authors and to arguments typical to Mumsnet. This could be carried out by evaluating the classifier on vaccine-related debate posts from other forums. The experimental design would then consist of using the Mumsnet data for the parameter setting and for training the models, and posts from other debate forums for evaluation.

6 Conclusion

A macro F-score of 0.62 was achieved for a binary classifier that distinguished debate posts taking a stance *against* vaccination from those taking a stance *for* vaccination. When also including the category *undecided*, an F-score of 0.44 was achieved for the three-class classifier. The detection of stance towards vaccination in online forums was proven to be a difficult task, at least for the support vector machine model trained on n-grams that was used as classifier and for the relatively small training corpus used. Future work will therefore include the expansion of the training data set, as well as an evaluation of other types of machine learning models and feature sets.

Acknowledgements

We would like to thank the reviewers for their valuable input. We would also like to thank the Swedish Research Council (Vetenskapsrådet) that funded this study, mainly through the project "Navigating in streams of opinions: Extracting and visualising arguments in opinionated texts" (No. 2016-06681) and partly through the StaViCTA project, framework grant "the Digitized Society – Past, Present, and Future" (No. 2012-5659).

References

Pranav Anand, Marilyn Walker, Rob Abbott, Jean E Fox Tree, Robeson Bowmani, and Michael Minor. 2011. Cats rule and dogs drool!: Classifying stance in online debate. In *Proceedings of the 2nd workshop on computational approaches to subjectivity and sentiment analysis*, pages 1–9, Stroudsburg, PA, USA. Association for Computational Linguistics.

Ron Artstein and Massimo Poesio. 2008. Inter-coder agreement for computational linguistics. *Comput. Linguist.*, 34(4):555–596.

Isabelle Augenstein, Tim Rocktäschel, Andreas Vlachos, and Kalina Bontcheva. 2016. Stance detection with bidirectional conditional encoding. In *Proceedings of the 2016 Conference on Empirical Methods in Natural Language Processing*, pages 876–885, Stroudsburg, PA, USA. Association for Computational Linguistics.

Steven Bird. 2002. Nltk: The natural language toolkit. In *Proceedings of the ACL Workshop on Effective Tools and Methodologies for Teaching Natural Language Processing and Computational Linguistics*, Stroudsburg, PA, USA. Association for Computational Linguistics.

Stephanie Brien, Nona Naderi, Arash Shaban-Nejad, Lukc Mondor, Doerthe Kroemker, and David L. Buckeridge. 2013. Vaccine attitude surveillance using semantic analysis: constructing a semantically annotated corpus. In *Proceddings of International*

World Wide Web Conference, IW3C2*, New York, NY, USA. ACM.

Helen Campbell, Angela Edwards, Louise Letley, Helen Bedford, Mary Ramsay, and Joanne Yarwood. 2017. Changing attitudes to childhood immunisation in english parents. *Vaccine*, 35(22):2979–2985.

Jingcheng Du, Jun Xu, Hsingyi Song, Xiangyu Liu, and Cui Tao. 2017. Optimization on machine learning based approaches for sentiment analysis on hpv vaccines related tweets. *J Biomed Semantics*, 8(1):9.

Fake News Challenge. 2017. Exploring how artificial intelligence technologies could be leveraged to combat fake news. http://www.fakenewschallenge.org, Accessed 2017-08-24.

William Ferreira and Andreas Vlachos. 2016. Emergent: a novel data-set for stance classification. In *Proceedings of the 2016 Conference of the North American Chapter of the Association for Computational Linguistics: Human Language Technologies, NAACL HLT*, Stroudsburg, PA, USA. Association for Computational Linguistics.

Kazi Saidul Hasan and Vincent Ng. 2013. Stance classification of ideological debates: Data, models, features, and constraints. In *International Joint Conference on Natural Language Processing, IJCNLP*, pages 1348–1356, Stroudsburg, PA, USA. Association for Computational Linguistics.

Heidi J Larson and Isaac Ghinai. 2011. Lessons from polio eradication. *Nature*, 473(7348):446–7.

Heidi J Larson, David M D Smith, Pauline Paterson, Melissa Cumming, Elisabeth Eckersberger, Clark C Freifeld, Isaac Ghinai, Caitlin Jarrett, Louisa Paushter, John S Brownstein, and Lawrence C Madoff. 2013. Measuring vaccine confidence: analysis of data obtained by a media surveillance system used to analyse public concerns about vaccines. *The Lancet Infectious Diseases*, 13(7).

Christopher D. Manning, Prabhakar Raghavan, and Hinrich Schütze. 2008. *Introduction to information retrieval*. Cambridge University Press, Cambridge.

Philip M Massey, Amy Leader, Elad Yom-Tov, Alexandra Budenz, Kara Fisher, and Ann C Klassen. 2016. Applying multiple data collection tools to quantify human papillomavirus vaccine communication on twitter. *J Med Internet Res*, 18(12):e318.

Caroline Modarressy-Tehrani. 2017. Anti-vaxxers and fear caused Minnesota's massive measles outbreak. *Vice news*.

Saif Mohammad, Parinaz Sobhani, and Svetlana Kiritchenko. 2017. Stance and sentiment in tweets. *ACM Transactions on Internet Technology (TOIT)*, 17(3):1–23.

Jan Pomikálek. 2011. *Removing boilerplate and duplicate content from web corpora*. Ph.D. thesis, Masaryk university, Faculty of informatics, Brno, Czech Republic.

Guido Powell, Kate Zinszer, Jahnavi Dhananjay, Chi Bahk, Lawrence C Madoff, John S Brownstein, Sabine Bergler, and David L Buckeridge. 2016a. Monitoring discussion of vaccine adverse events in the media: Opportunities from the vaccine sentimeter. In *AAAI Workshop: WWW and Population Health Intelligence*, Palo Alto, California, USA. Association for the Advancement of Artificial Intelligence.

Guido Antonio Powell, Kate Zinszer, Aman Verma, Chi Bahk, Lawrence Madoff, John Brownstein, and David Buckeridge. 2016b. Media content about vaccines in the united states and canada, 2012-2014: An analysis using data from the vaccine sentimeter. *Vaccine*, 34(50):6229–6235.

Marcel Salathé and Shashank Khandelwal. 2011. Assessing vaccination sentiments with online social media: implications for infectious disease dynamics and control. *PLoS Comput Biol*, 7(10):e1002199.

Zoë C Skea, Vikki A Entwistle, Ian Watt, and Elizabeth Russell. 2008. 'Avoiding harm to others' considerations in relation to parental measles, mumps and rubella (MMR) vaccination discussions - an analysis of an online chat forum. *Soc Sci Med*, 67(9):1382–90.

Swapna Somasundaran and Janyce Wiebe. 2010. Recognizing stances in ideological on-line debates. In *Proceedings of the NAACL HLT 2010 Workshop on Computational Approaches to Analysis and Generation of Emotion in Text*, CAAGET '10, pages 116–124, Stroudsburg, PA, USA. Association for Computational Linguistics.

Timothy R Tangherlini, Vwani Roychowdhury, Beth Glenn, Catherine M Crespi, Roja Bandari, Akshay Wadia, Misagh Falahi, Ehsan Ebrahimzadeh, and Roshan Bastani. 2016. "Mommy blogs" and the vaccination exemption narrative: Results from a machine-learning approach for story aggregation on parenting social media sites. *JMIR Public Health Surveill*, 2(2):e166.

Marilyn A. Walker, Pranav Anand, Robert Abbott, and Ricky Grant. 2012. Stance classification using dialogic properties of persuasion. In *Proceedings of the 2012 Conference of the North American Chapter of the Association for Computational Linguistics: Human Language Technologies*, NAACL HLT '12, pages 592–596, Stroudsburg, PA, USA. Association for Computational Linguistics.

Analysing the Causes of Depressed Mood from Depression Vulnerable Individuals

Noor Fazilla Abd Yusof, Chenghua Lin and **Frank Guerin**
Computing Science, University of Aberdeen, Aberdeen UK
{noorfazilla.yusof, chenghua.lin, f.guerin}@abdn.ac.uk

Abstract

We develop a computational model to discover the potential causes of depression by analysing the topics from user-generated contents. We show the most prominent causes, and how these causes evolve over time. Also, we highlight the differences in causes between students with low and high neuroticism. Our studies demonstrate that the topics reveal valuable clues about the causes contributing to depressed mood. Identifying causes can have a significant impact on improving the quality of depression care; thereby providing greater insights into a patient's state for pertinent treatment recommendations. Hence, this study significantly expands the ability to discover the potential factors that trigger depression, making it possible to increase the efficiency of depression treatment.

1 Introduction

Depression is one of the most common mental disorders that can affect people of all ages. It is the leading cause of disability and requires significant health care cost to treat effectively (Smith et al., 2013). Early detection and treatment has a profound impact to encourage remission, and prevent relapse (Halfin, 2007). However, it is rather common that the stigma associated with mental illness makes patients reluctant to seek help, or makes them tend to answer questions in a manner that will be viewed favourable by the clinician (Chandra and Minkovitz, 2006). In addition, clinical diagnosis depends on the hypothetical or retrospective self-reports of behaviour, requiring patients to reflect on what they were doing and thinking sometime in the past, which may have become obscured over time. Hence, it is difficult for physicians to capture first-hand the patients' own experiences, an important factor for diagnosis and providing the most appropriate treatment at the point of care (Kosinski et al., 2015).

Social media sites provide great venues for people to share their experiences, vent emotion and stress, and seek social support. Therefore, mental health studies based on social media present several advantages (Inkster et al., 2016). For instance, these digital footprints contain vast amounts of implicit knowledge, which are useful for medical practitioners to understand patients' experiences outside the controlled clinical environment. In addition, information captured during clinical consultation generally reflects only the situation of the patient at the time of care. In contrast, data collected from social media is dynamic, thereby providing opportunities for observing and recognising critical changes in patients' behaviour and permitting certain interventions in real time (Inkster et al., 2016).

Due to the advantages identified above, social media and natural language processing techniques are increasingly used in a wide range of mental health related studies. This includes works that can detect (Coppersmith et al., 2014; Resnik et al., 2015) and measure the degree of depression (Schwartz et al., 2014), identify depressive symptoms (Mowery et al., 2016), and detect the behavioural changes associated with onset of depression (De Choudhury et al., 2013b). There are also works focus on predicting personality traits such as neuroticism (Resnik et al., 2013), which is known to be highly associated with depression.

However, the above mentioned works mainly focus on recognising depression, with the potential causes of depression being ignored. Discovering the potential causes of depression is a worthwhile aspect of psychiatric diagnosis in order to offer the individual patient with solution-

Proceedings of the International Workshop on Digital Disease Detection using Social Media 2017 (DDDSM-2017), pages 9–17,
Taipei, Taiwan, November 27, 2017.

specific, interpersonal or psychodynamic therapy for the best treatment outcome (Nathan and Gorman, 2015). For example, interpersonal psychotherapy can benefit patients who have recognised interpersonal problems as the cause of their depression. Furthermore, identifying causes can improve the efficiency of the treatment plan, as it is normally involved in a patient's diagnostic evaluation and can help recognise possible barriers to treatment support (Gilman et al., 2013).

In this paper, we tackle the research challenge of discovering potential causes of depression by analysing the topics from user-generated contents. We approach the problem by developing a computational model which extends the dynamic topic model (He et al., 2012). In order to extract coherent sentiment-bearing topics that are indicative for identifying the causes of depression, we develop the major categories of depression cause based on two well-known resources i.e., DSM-IV (Gilman et al., 2013) and Crisis Text Line (`www.crisistextline.org`). We also propose a mechanism to incorporate domain knowledge of depression causes into our model for guiding the model inference procedure, which helps us to extract depression related and meaningful topics. Experimental results show that our approach can extract topics revealing valuable clues and risk factors about the causes contributing to depression based on informal user-generated data; thereby providing deep insights into a patient's state for pertinent treatment recommendations.

2 Related Work

A wide range of risk factors are associated with the development and persistence of depression (e.g., biological, psychological or cognitive), however, psychosocial are among the strongest (Slavich and Irwin, 2014). To examine depressive disorder, one effective means is via language analysis, as the use of language can be linked to important information about people's behaviours and psychological insights (Pennebaker et al., 2003).

De Choudhury et al. (2013a) showed that Support Vector Machines (SVM) with Radial Basis Function (RBF) kernel could predict depression signs from Twitter posts. A similar approach was applied to Japanese Twitter posts for investigating the correlations between users' activities and depression (Tsugawa et al., 2015). Coppersmith et al. (2014) used language models and Linguistic Inquiry Word Count (LIWC) (Pennebaker et al., 2007), a psychometrically validated analysis tool, to explore the language differences of Post-Traumatic Stress Disorder users. Schwartz et al. (2014) built a regression model to predict the degree of depression across seasons based on language features on Facebook.

In contrast to the works above which analyse static data, there has also been research in examining changes in behavioural patterns relating to onset of depression. For instance, De Choudhury and Counts (2013) analysed the behavioural changes of new mothers who are at risk of postpartum depression following childbirth. In the subsequent work, De Choudhury et al. (2013b) further predicted whether one is likely to have depression in the future by examining the patterns of one's Twitter postings in a one-year time frame. Both studies showed that significant changes in social media activities could be the potential measures for predicting depression.

Another stream of works employ the Big Five personality traits (John and Srivastava, 1999) in depressive illness related studies. The Big Five personality traits define five different personality characteristics i.e., *extroversion*, *agreeableness*, *conscientiousness*, *neuroticism*, and *openness*. Among these personal traits, neuroticism is known to have a substantial correlation to the prior development of common depressive illness and psychological distress (Fanous et al., 2007). Schwartz et al. (2013) explored an open-vocabulary approach to gain psychological insights based on the demographics and personality traits framework. The works of Resnik et al. (2013, 2015) are most closely related to ours, as they explored topic modelling to automatically identify depressive-related language. They showed that using topic models provides better predictive performance than solely relying on pre-defined lexical features. They also highlighted that the topics extracted by Latent Dirichlet Allocation (LDA) (Blei et al., 2003) are meaningful and psychologically relevant. Specifically, Resnik et al. (2013) combined lexical features with features extracted by topic models, which improves the prediction of neuroticism and depression on student essay data. In the more recent work, Resnik et al. (2015) further explored using Supervised LDA (Mcauliffe and Blei, 2008) and Supervised Anchor model (Arora et al., 2013) to analyse the linguistic signal for detecting depression.

To the best of our knowledge, no studies have explored the research problem of automatically identifying the causes of depression using natural language processing techniques. We envisage that by addressing this problem, our work would be useful for both individual and population-level mental health monitoring and prevention.

3 Methodology

In this section, we first describe how we acquire the categories of causes of depression, and then describe the computational framework for automatically extracting coherent topics that are indicative for identifying the causes of depression.

3.1 Development of Cause Categories for Depression

For extracting potential causes of depression from text, we first develop the major categories of depression cause based on two well-known resources.

First, we construct the primary list based on the risk factors outlined in the description of Axis IV in DSM-IV (Gilman et al., 2013). DSM-IV is a standard diagnostic manual of mental disorders, which defines nine broad categories that increase the risk of developing depression. The broad categories include problems related to *primary support group*, *social environment*, *occupational*, *economic*, *educational*, *housing*, *accessing to health-care services*, and *legal/crime*. However, some of the categories are too broad or do not state precisely enough for the causes, such as "primary support group" and "social environment". Therefore, in order to obtain a more comprehensive list of depression causes, we further make use of the resources available from Crisis Text Line[1].

Basically, Crisis Text Line is one of the largest crisis counselling services which supports a wide range of issues from relationship concerns to depression to suicidal thoughts. We utilise the trends list of 17 issues prevalent to depression: *anxiety*, *bereavement*, *bullying*, *eating disorders*, *family issues*, *friend issues*, *health concerns*, *isolations*, *LGBT issues*, *physical abuse*, *relationships*, *school problems*, *self-harm*, *sexual abuse*, *stress*, *substance abuse*, and *suicidal thoughts*.

To ensure the quality of the cause categories developed based on the above resources, we also consulted a physician who had an extensive experiences dealing with depression cases. We worked together to refine the list, taking into consideration the leading factors contributing to depression. We discarded the ones which are not quite related to the causes of depression, i.e., suicidal thoughts and self-harm. We also added to the list two other common issues that reinforce negative thoughts or emotions. For instance, body image (e.g. body-hatred, overweight, underweight) and homesickness have been considered associated with psychological disturbance, especially among young adults.

We present the categories of depression causes in Table 1. While this is by no means an explicit list of causes of depression. Indeed, there can be as many different causes of depression as possible. Our argument that this is an initial development and we account for their relative significance. The list can be extended in our future research.

Bullying	Family issues
Housing	Health concerns
Body image	Substance abuse
Bereavement	Occupation
Homesickness	Academic
Relationships	Economic
Discrimination	Sexual abuse
Physical abuse	

Table 1: Depression cause categories.

3.2 The dynamic Joint Sentiment-Topic model

We employ the dynamic Joint Sentiment-Topic (dJST) model (He et al., 2012) to extract coherent sentiment-bearing topics that are indicative for identifying the causes of depression. In addition, the model is also capable to track how the topics evolve over time, permitting investigation of the prominence of depression causes.

The dJST model, as shown in Figure 1, assumes that the current sentiment-topic words distributions are generated by the word distributions at the previous epochs. Each document d at epoch t is represented as a vector of word tokens, $w_d^t = (w_{d_1}^t, w_{d_2}^t, \cdots, w_{d_{N_d}}^t)$. By assuming that the documents at current epoch are influenced by documents at past, the current sentiment-topic specific word distributions $\varphi_{l,z}^t$ at epoch t are generated according to the word distribu-

[1]www.crisistrends.org

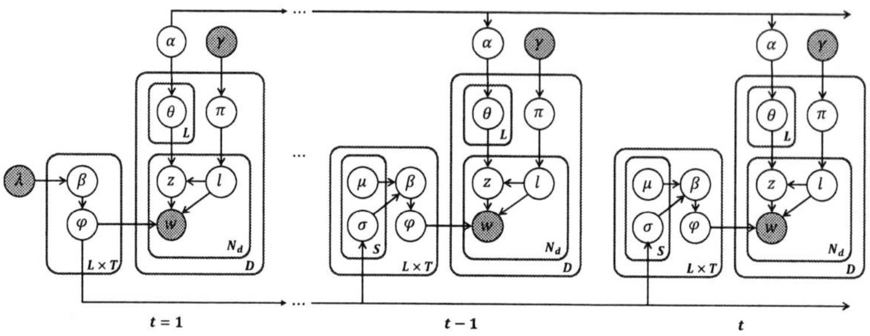

Figure 1: dJST model.

tions at previous epochs. In particular, an evolutionary matrix of topic z and sentiment label l, $E^t_{l,z}$ where each column in the matrix is the word distribution of topic z and sentiment label l, $\sigma^t_{l,z,s}$, generated for document streams received within the time slice specified by s, where $s \in \{t-S, t-S+1, \cdots, t-1\}$, the current sentiment-topic-word distributions are dependent on the previous sentiment-topic specific word distributions in the last S epochs.

We then attach a vector of S weights $\boldsymbol{\mu}^t_{l,z} = [\mu^t_{l,z,0}, \mu^t_{l,z,1}, \cdots, \mu^t_{l,z,S}]^{\mathrm{T}}$, each of which determines the contribution of time slice s in computing the priors of $\varphi^t_{l,z}$. Hence, the Dirichlet prior for sentiment-topic-word distributions at epoch t is $\beta^t_{l,z} = \boldsymbol{E}^{t-1}_{l,z}\boldsymbol{\mu}^t_{l,z}$. Assuming we have already calculated the evolutionary parameters $\{\boldsymbol{E}^{t-1}_{l,z}, \boldsymbol{\mu}^t_{l,z}\}$ for the current epoch t, the generative story of dJST as shown in Figure 1 at epoch t is given as follows:

- For each sentiment label $l = 1, \cdots, L$
  - For each topic $z = 1, \cdots, T$
    * Draw $\alpha^t_{l,z}|\alpha^{t-1}_{l,z} \sim \Gamma(\nu\alpha^{t-1}_{l,z}, \nu)$
    * Compute $\beta^t_{l,z} = \mu^t_{l,z}E^t_{l,z}$
    * Draw $\varphi^t_{l,z} \sim \mathrm{Dir}(\beta^t_{l,z})$.
- For each document $d = 1, \cdots, D^t$
  - Choose a distribution $\pi^t_d \sim \mathrm{Dir}(\gamma)$.
  - For each sentiment label l under document d, choose a distribution $\theta^t_{d,l} \sim \mathrm{Dir}(\sigma^t)$.
  - For each word $n = 1, \cdots, N_d$ in document d
    * Choose a sentiment label $l_n \sim \mathrm{Mult}(\pi^t_d)$,
    * Choose a topic $z_n \sim \mathrm{Mult}(\theta^t_{d,ln})$,
    * Choose a word $w_n \sim \mathrm{Mult}(\varphi^t_{ln,zn})$.

3.2.1 Incorporating Domain Knowledge

In order to extract depression cause relevant and semantically meaningful topics, we incorporate two types of domain knowledge into our model for guiding the model inference procedure.

The first type of domain knowledge is a general sentiment lexicon consists of the Multi-perspective Question Answering (MPQA) subjectivity lexicon[2] and the appraisal lexicon (Bloom et al., 2007). In total, there are 1,511 positive and 2,542 negative words, respectively. The second type of domain knowledge is seed words relating to depression cause categories described in Section 3.1. To acquire the seed words, we make use of OneLook Dictionary[3], a search engine for words and phrases. Precisely, for each of the depression category, we query OneLook by searching for words related to the depression cause category label. For instance, for category "bullying", we obtain 539 words related to bullying e.g., *intimidation, harrasment, brutal*, etc. We filter and retain the top 50 most relevant words to the search query. We use those words to be the seed words as prior knowledge for the model training. The total number of seed words contains 750 words.

At epoch 1, the Dirichlet priors β of size $L \times T \times V$ are first initialized as symmetric priors of 0.01 (Steyvers and Griffiths, 2007), and then modified by a transformation matrix $\boldsymbol{\lambda}$ of size $L \times V$. We encode the word prior knowledge in the way that elements of β corresponding to positive sentiment words, e.g., *good*, will have small values for topics associated with negative sentiment labels, and vice versa for the negative sentiment words. For subsequent epochs, if any new words encountered, the prior knowledge will be incorporated in a similar way. But for existing words, their

[2] `http://www.cs.pitt.edu/mpqa/`
[3] `https://www.onelook.com`

Dirichlet priors for sentiment-topic-word distributions are obtained using $\beta^t_{l,z} = \boldsymbol{E}^{t-1}_{l,z}\boldsymbol{\mu}^t_{l,z}$.

3.2.2 Online Inference

We employ a stochastic EM algorithm (He et al., 2012) to sequentially update model parameters at each epoch. At each EM iteration, we infer latent sentiment labels and topics using the collapsed Gibbs sampling and estimate the hyperparameters using maximum likelihood.

We set the symmetric prior $\gamma = (0.05 \times \text{average document length})/L$, where L is the total number of sentiment labels and the value of 0.05 on average allocates 5% of probability mass for mixing. Moreover, there are two sets of evolutionary parameters to be estimated, the weight parameters $\boldsymbol{\mu}$ and the evolutionary matrix $\boldsymbol{E}$. We set $\boldsymbol{\mu}$ using an exponential decay function $\boldsymbol{\mu}^t = \exp(-\kappa t)$, so that more recent documents would have a relatively stronger influence on the model parameters in the current epoch compared to earlier documents. We set $\kappa = 0.5$ in the experiments. The derivation of the evolutionary matrix $\boldsymbol{E}$ requires the estimation of each of its elements, $\sigma_{l,z,w,s}$, i.e., the word distribution of word w in topic z and sentiment label l at time slice s, which is defined as $\sigma^t_{l,z,w,s} = \frac{C^t_{l,z,w,s}}{\sum_w C^t_{l,z,w,s}}$. Here $C_{l,z,w,s}$ is the expected number of times word w was assigned to sentiment label l and topic z at time slice s. Each time slice s is equivalent to an epoch t, thus $C_{l,z,w,s}$ can be obtained directly from $N_{l,z,w,t}$ by setting $s = t$.

4 Experimental Setup

Dataset. We conducted experiments on a real-world dataset, namely, the student essay dataset. This dataset is publicly available and has been used in a number of mental health studies (Resnik et al., 2013). It contains 6,459 stream-of-consciousness essays collected between 1997 and 2008, and each essay is labelled with Big-5 personality traits scores. As discussed earlier, neuroticism (negative affectivity) is a factor that strongly associates with high risk of depressive disorders. We divided the dataset into two categories based on the neuroticism scores, i.e, essays with positive scores are classified as high neuroticism, and negative score as low neuroticism. Any essays missing personality traits scores were eliminated from the dataset. The final dataset contains a total number of 4,954 essays with 2,566 associated with high neuroticism and 2,388 associated with low neuroticism, as shown in Figure 2.

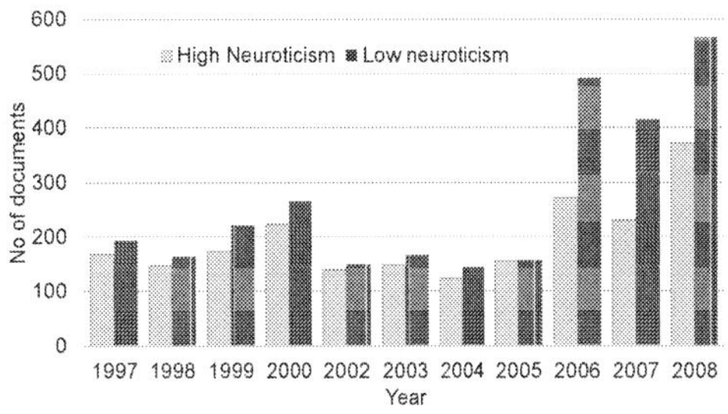

Figure 2: Number of stream-of-consciousness essays over 11 years (1997-2008).

General Settings. Each dataset underwent preprocessing including conversion to lowercase, removal of non-alphanumeric characters, and removal of stop words. We empirically set the number of topics to 20 for the 2 sentiment labels (i.e., positive and negative), which is equivalent to a total of 40 sentiment-topic clusters. The number of time-slices set to 4.

5 Experimental Results

In this section, we present our results on the experimental datasets. In particular, we aim to investigate the following two research questions: (i) what are the most prominent causes for neuroticism among college students and how do these causes evolve over time; and (ii) what are the differences of the topics extracted from essays written by of students from low and high neuroticism groups.

5.1 Analysing the Depressing-related Issues from the High Neurotisism Group

In this section, we present the results on extracting topics for depression-related causes analysis. Figure 3 illustrates the example topics from high neuroticism (negative sentiment) and low neuroticism (positive sentiment). The topics extracted are in agreement with those reported in the risk factors that contribute to stress experienced by students (Robotham and Julian, 2006). We discuss some of the topics in details below.

Academic. Unsurprisingly, one of the prominent causes among the students with high-neuroticism score is related to academic studies, consistent with the report of primary causes of stress among

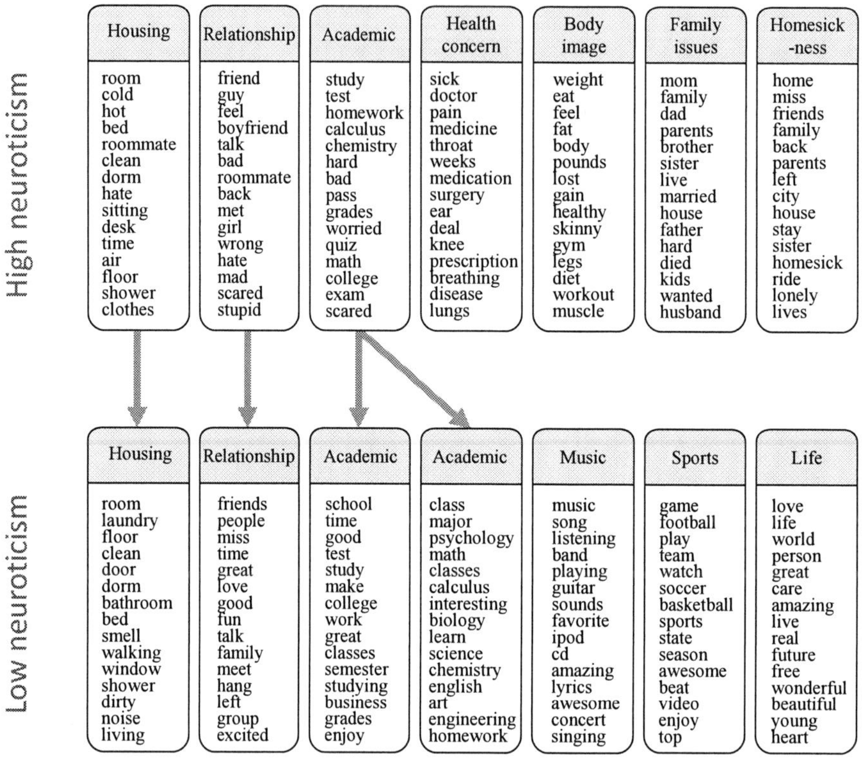

Figure 3: Example topics from high and low neuroticism. The upper panels show the topics under negative sentiment (high neuroticism); the lower panel under positive sentiment (low neuroticism). Note: The connecting arrows describe the sentiment differences towards the same topic theme.

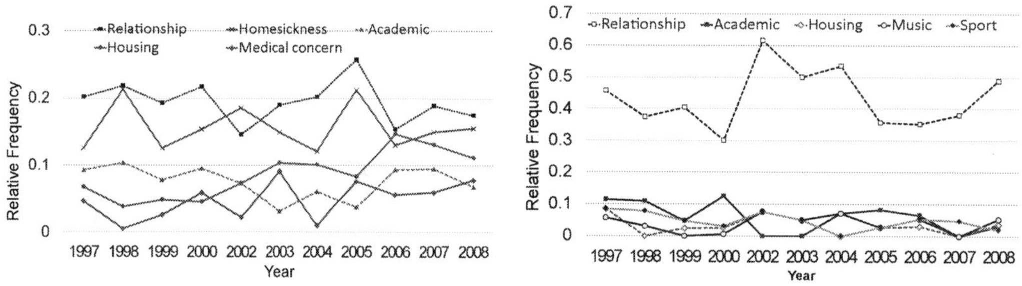

(a) (b)

Figure 4: Frequency distribution of top 5 sentiment topics across years (a) High neuroticism; (b) Low neuroticism.

students[4]. `Academic` topic words in Figure 3 (e.g., "*study, test, bad, grades, worried*") show that students express a very stressful experiences in study. For example, "*I am scared that my grades won't be able to cut it though*", "*I am pretty much worried about my classes and what grades I will get in them*".

Relationship and homesickness. Our analysis found that relationship problems and homesickness are also widely common among stu-

[4]https://yougov.co.uk/news/2016/08/09/quarter-britains-students-are-afflicted-mental-hea/

dents, as shown in the `Relationship` and `Homesickness` topics. Indeed, intimate relationships with a partner can be a great source of love, support and excitement. However, relationships can also be a source of grief and anguish if they go wrong. University students are in a period of personal change, which can then make them feel less sure or what they want or how to cope with relationship problems. For examples, *"I feel insecure about our relationship myself and in some way feel like I am not worthy of someone liking me"*. Research by the National Union of Students[5] shows that 50-70% of new students suffer from homesickness to some extent within in their first two or three weeks. Although most students find their symptoms begin to fade after a few weeks, the symptoms tend to stay longer for students with high neuroticism.

Housing. Another interesting finding is that bad accommodation seems to have strong negative impact on the socio-emotional development and psychological distress of students. For instance, there are lot of complaint about the condition of the university accommodation, e.g., *"Someone in this room needs to buy a mop because our floor is getting really gross"*, *"Our shower is very small in the first place and combined with being dirty, well that's just plain bad"*. There is a strong link of mental health problems with insecure, and the chaotic way of living (Tight, 2011).

Body image and health concerns. Individuals with high level of neuroticism seem less satisfied with their body image and health as implied in topics `Body Image` and `Health concerns`. For instance, messages similar to *"I am so nervous about gaining weight. I always watch what i eat"* appear quite often in the dataset. This shows that physiological factors do promote to dissatisfaction in students' life, which lead to low self-esteem (correlated with high neuroticism).

5.2 Comparing the High and the Low Neuroticism Groups.

We estimate the probability of top 5 topics across years using the relative frequency technique. We calculate the 'relative observed frequencies' of a topic, and divide the number of occurrences of the topic by the number of documents for that particular year. Figure 4 shows the distribution of top 5 topics of high and low neuroticism. We found that the topic `Relationship` is very common among students from both groups. The trend reflects the fact that students are prone to stress in student life, often caused by the poor relationship issues, which also lead to struggles in academic, social adjustment, and individual self-esteem.

Another interesting key difference to highlight is on the social engagement level. Students with low neuroticism are much more active and show more interest in various social activities (e.g., music and sports). Similar findings are consistent with research (Afshar et al., 2015), in that the individuals with low-neuroticism are more likely to utilise relaxation (music, meditation, yoga, etc.) and physical recreation (regular exercise, sports, running, etc.) as coping mechanisms.

Sentiment analysis. We discuss the sentiment differences on the same topic between two groups, as shown in Figure 3. The topics about academic and relationship are both prominent among these groups, however, there are differences in perceptions and emotional reactivity towards these topics. Specifically, students with high-neuroticism respond poorly to environmental stress and interpret ordinary situations as threatening and experience minor frustrations as hopelessly overwhelming. For example, they seem to have difficulty in coping the issues and challenges from academic studies. Below are some examples,

- *"I hate myself for not doing well in some other class. Its a vicious cycle that I can't seem to get out of. I do bad in one class because I focus on all the wrong things and then it carries over to ever other class, which in turn makes my academics suffer"*.
- *"I'm worried about studying for psychology. It's my first collegiate test. I'll probably do terrible. or at least far less than my expectations"*.

Whereas, students with low neuroticism seem to have higher stress tolerance when dealing with academic pressures. They are more resilient to challenges, embrace and overcome obstacles in a positive way. Take for examples the following,

- *"I am eager for the future and ecstatic for what is yet to come. I hope I am joining the right organizations that appeal to me. I also hope I will stay academically strong as I was in high school"*.
- *"Its going to be my first official test in college. I just can't imagine me taking a test. I just need to relax, study the best I can, and be optimistic about my academics"*.

[5] `https://www.nus.org.uk/`

6 Conclusion

The causes of depression can vary greatly from person to person. It is a great challenge for clinical practice in the recognition and treatment of depression, particularly when there are barriers in getting the appropriate support, e.g., time constraints in primary care, a strong social stigma attached to mental illness and discrimination. Our approach on topic modelling for classification certainly bridges the gap and significantly expands the access in identifying the possible factors that trigger depression in individuals. Identifying the causes of depression increases the accuracy of selecting the most appropriate treatment and improves the quality of depression care. Therefore, further research should be undertaken to optimise topic models for drawing out potential causes of depression from social media data. Furthermore, a dataset with ground truth that covers wider causes of depression such as financial and occupation should be explored in the future, to cater for different groups of people e.g., employee, housewives, etc.

Acknowledgments

This work is supported by the awards made by the UK Engineering and Physical Sciences Research Council (Grant number: EP/P005810/1). Lead author would like to thank Ministry of Higher Education Malaysia and Technical University of Malaysia Malacca for PhD scholarship award.

References

H Afshar, H Roohafza, A Keshteli, M Mazaheri, A Feizi, and P Adibi. 2015. The association of personality traits and coping styles according to stress level. *IJRMS* 20(4):353.

S Arora, R Ge, Y Halpern, D Mimno, A Moitra, D Sontag, Y Wu, and M Zhu. 2013. A Practical Algorithm for Topic Modeling with Provable Guarantees. In *Int. Conf. Mach. Learn.*. pages 280–288.

D Blei, Andrew Ng, and M Jordan. 2003. Latent dirichlet allocation. *Journal of machine Learning research* 3(Jan):993–1022.

K Bloom, S Stein, and S Argamon. 2007. Appraisal extraction for news opinion analysis at NTCIR-6. In *Proc. NTCIR-6, National Institute of Informatics*.

A Chandra and C Minkovitz. 2006. Stigma starts early: Gender differences in teen willingness to use mental health services. *J. Adolesc. Heal.* 38(6):754–e1.

G Coppersmith, C Harman, and M Dredze. 2014. Measuring Post Traumatic Stress Disorder in Twitter. In *Proc. ICWSM*. pages 579–582.

M De Choudhury and Sand Horvitz E Counts. 2013. Predicting postpartum changes in emotion and behavior via social media. In *Proc. SIGCHI-13*. pages 3267–3276.

M De Choudhury, S Counts, and E Horvitz. 2013a. Social media as a measurement tool of depression in populations. In *Proc. ACM WebSci*. pages 47–56.

M De Choudhury, M Gamon, S Counts, and E Horvitz. 2013b. Predicting Depression via Social Media. In *Proc. ICWSM*. volume 2, page 2.

A Fanous, M Neale, S Aggen, and K Kendler. 2007. A longitudinal study of personality and major depression in a population-based sample of male twins. *Psychol. Med.* 37(08):1163.

S Gilman, N Trinh, J Smoller, M Fava, J Murphy, and J Breslau. 2013. Psychosocial stressors and the prognosis of major depression: a test of Axis IV. *Psychol. Med.* 43(2):303–316.

A Halfin. 2007. Depression: the benefits of early and appropriate treatment. *Am. J. Manag. Care* 13(4 Suppl):S92–7.

Y He, C Lin, and A Cano. 2012. Online sentiment and topic dynamics tracking over the streaming data. In *Int. Conf. Soc. Comput.*. pages 258–266.

B Inkster, D Stillwell, M Kosinski, and P Jones. 2016. A decade into Facebook: where is psychiatry in the digital age? *Lancet Psychiatry* 3(11):1087–1090.

O John and S Srivastava. 1999. The Big Five trait taxonomy: History, measurement, and theoretical perspectives. *Handb. Personal. Theory Res.* 2(1999):102–138.

M Kosinski, S Matz, S Gosling, V Popov, and D Stillwell. 2015. Facebook as a research tool for the social sciences: Opportunities, challenges, ethical considerations, and practical guidelines. *Am. Psychol.* 70(6):543–556.

J Mcauliffe and D Blei. 2008. Supervised topic models. In *Adv. Neural Inf. Process. Syst.*. Curran Associates, Inc., pages 121–128.

D Mowery, A Park, M Conway, and B Craig. 2016. Towards Automatically Classifying Depressive Symptoms from Twitter Data for Population Health. In *Proc. PEOPLES 2016*. pages 182–191.

P Nathan and J Gorman. 2015. *A guide to treatments that work*. Oxford University Press.

J Pennebaker, C Chung, M Ireland, A Gonzales, and R Booth. 2007. The development and psychometric properties of liwc2007: Liwc. net.

J Pennebaker, M Mehl, and K Niederhoffer. 2003. Psychological aspects of natural language use: Our words, our selves. *Annu. Rev. Psychol.* 54(1):547–577.

P Resnik, W Armstrong, L Claudino, T Nguyen, V Nguyen, and J Boyd-graber. 2015. Beyond LDA : Exploring Supervised Topic Modeling for Depression-Related Language in Twitter. In *Proc. CLPsych*. volume 1, pages 99–107.

P Resnik, A Garron, and R Resnik. 2013. Using Topic Modeling to Improve Prediction of Neuroticism and Depression in College Students. In *Proc. EMNLP*. pages 1348–1353.

D Robotham and C Julian. 2006. Stress and the higher education student: a critical review of the literature. *J. Furth. High. Educ.* 30(2):107–117.

H Schwartz, J Eichstaedt, M Kern, L Dziurzynski, S Ramones, M Agrawal, A Shah, M Kosinski, D Stillwell, M Seligman, and L Ungar. 2013. Personality, Gender, and Age in the Language of Social Media: The Open-Vocabulary Approach. *PLoS One* 8(9):e73791.

H Schwartz, J Eichstaedt, M Kern, G Park, M Sap, D Stillwell, M Kosinski, and L Ungar. 2014. Towards Assessing Changes in Degree of Depression through Facebook. In *Proc. CLPsych*. pages 118–125.

G Slavich and M Irwin. 2014. From stress to inflammation and major depressive disorder: A social signal transduction theory of depression. *Psychol. Bull.* 140(3):774.

K Smith, P Renshaw, and J Bilello. 2013. The diagnosis of depression: Current and emerging methods. *Compr. Psychiatry* 54(1):1–6.

M Steyvers and T Griffiths. 2007. Probabilistic topic models. *Handb. Latent Semant. Anal.* 427(7):424–440.

M Tight. 2011. Student accommodation in higher education in the United Kingdom: changing postwar attitudes. *Oxford Rev. Educ.* 37(1):109–122.

S Tsugawa, Y Kikuchi, F Kishino, K Nakajima, Y Itoh, and H Ohsaki. 2015. Recognizing Depression from Twitter Activity. In *Proc. ACM CHI*. pages 3187–3196.

Multivariate Linear Regression of Symptoms-related Tweets for Infectious Gastroenteritis Scale Estimation

Ryo Takeuchi, Hayate Iso, Kaoru Ito, Shoko Wakamiya, Eiji Aramaki
{takeuchi.ryo.tj7, iso.hayate.id3, kito, wakamiya, aramaki}@is.naist.jp

Abstract

To date, various Twitter-based event detection systems have been proposed. Most of their targets, however, share common characteristics. They are seasonal or global events such as earthquakes and flu pandemics. In contrast, this study targets unseasonal and local disease events. Our system investigates the frequencies of disease-related words such as "*nausea*," "*chill*," and "*diarrhea*" and estimates the number of patients using regression of these word frequencies. Experiments conducted using Japanese 47 areas from January 2017 to April 2017 revealed that the detection of small and unseasonal event is extremely difficult (r = 0.13). However, we found that the event scale and the detection performance show high correlation in the specified cases (in the phase of patient increasing or decreasing). The results also suggest that when 150 and more patients appear in a high population area, we can expect that our social sensors detect this outbreak. Based on these results, we can infer that social sensors can reliably detect unseasonal and local disease events under certain conditions, just as they can for seasonal or global events.

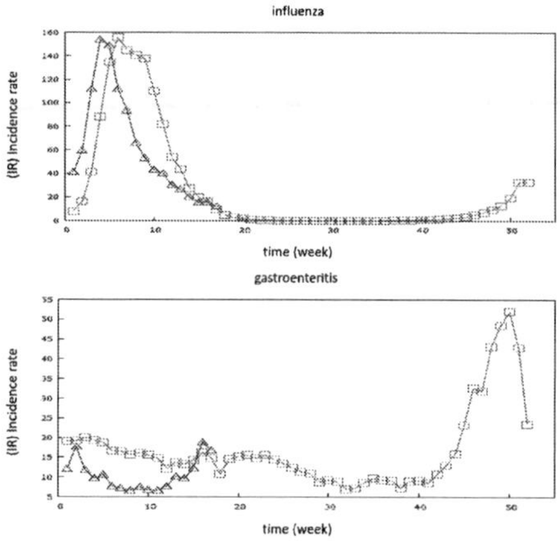

Figure 1: Seasonal global event (a) vs. Unseasonal local event (b). The X-axis shows the timeline (weekly based). The Y-axis shows the incidence rate (IR), corresponding to the patient number per area during the latest two years. Thin line with red square markers show the incidence rates of 2016. The line with blue triangle markers show the incidence rates of 2017. (a) Seasonal global event (*Influenza* in Japan). The *influenza* portrays a single big peak. (b) Unseasonal local event *Gastroenteritis* in the same area as (a). The *Gastroenteritis* shows numerous small peaks. It is difficult to detect Peak periods.

1 Introduction

Nowadays, the concept of *social sensors* (Sakaki et al., 2010) has been shown to have great potential feasibility for various practical applications. Particularly, disease detection is a core target of social sensor based studies. To date, detection has been demonstrated for influenza (Aramaki et al., 2011; Paul et al., 2014; Lampos et al., 2015; Iso et al., 2016; Wakamiya et al., 2016; Zhang et al., 2017; Lampos et al., 2017), E.Coli (Diaz-Aviles and Stewart, 2012), and H1N1-type flu (Culotta, 2013; Lampos and Cristianini, 2010).

In this field, infectious diseases have drawn much attention mainly for the following two reasons. First, from a practical perspective, infectious disease prevention is a crucially important mission for a nation because infectious diseases, especially influenza, cause many deaths and spread rapidly. Next, from the perspective of informatics, epidemics of these diseases are suitable targets because some epidemics have the following characteristics that make them easy to ascertain from

Proceedings of the International Workshop on Digital Disease Detection using Social Media 2017 (DDDSM-2017), pages 18–25,
Taipei, Taiwan, November 27, 2017. ©2017 AFNLP

social media:

1. **Seasonal Event**: some epidemics are seasonal diseases that have basically one big peak during one year (e.g. influenza).

2. **Large Scale Event**: some epidemics infect thousands of people. Accordingly, the scale of information related to the disease in twitter also becomes large (e.g. more than 100,000 flu-related Japanese tweets per day).

Compared with previous works, this study tackles a more challenging task: detection of outbreaks of *infectious gastroenteritis* (In the rest of the paper, we simply call it *gastroenteritis*). Outbreaks of gastroenteritis are often caused by viruses such as *Norovirus* and *Campylobacter*. Symptoms include some combinations of various hard complaints, diarrhea, vomiting, and abdominal pain, fever, and dehydration, which typically last less than two weeks. These features of gastroenteritis make the task more difficult: unlike the flu, the name of a particular disease agent is rarely tweeted. The increased number of patients must be estimated with tweets related to several symptoms.

Although gastroenteritis is sometimes called *stomach flu*, the gastroenteritis characteristics in social respects show quite a contrast to the flu.

1. **Unseasonal Event**: An outbreak of gastroenteritis is not seasonal. It can burst at any time of a year. Moreover, there can be many peaks during a single year.

2. **Local Event**: The scale of the gastroenteritis varies, starting from a smaller event involving a couple of patients to a larger event involving thousands of patients.

A comparison of influenza and gastroenteritis is presented in Figure 1. These characteristics also make it difficult to apply a method intended for influenza detection to gastroenteritis detection.

This study investigates the estimation performance for smaller events rather than previous targets. The results reveal that the event size is a core factor affecting the social sensor performance. From experimentally obtained results, small events (related to about 150 people) were detected with high accuracy (the correlation ratio between social sensor estimation and the actual value is 0.8).

This result contributes to social sensor reliability. This paper is the first reporting the overall relation between social sensor performance and its factors. Although detection of small and unseasonal events is difficult, the sensor can be applied in specified situations.

2 Related Work

Detection of infectious diseases is an important part of national health control. Detection tasks are classifiable into two types: (1) Seasonal infection for diseases such as influenza, and (2) Unseasonal infection such as food poisoning (infectious gastroenteritis) and bio-terror attacks.

For the earliest possible detection, most countries have infection prevention centers: The U.S. has the Centers for Disease Control and Prevention (CDC). The E.U. has its European Influenza Surveillance Scheme (EISS). Japan has its Infection Disease Surveillance Center (IDSC). For each of them, surveillance systems rely on virology and clinical data. For instance, the IDSC gathers influenza patient data from 5,000 clinics and releases summary reports. Such manual systems typically have a 1–2 week reporting lag, which is sometimes pointed out as a major flaw.

In an attempt to provide earlier infectious detection, various new approaches have been proposed to date, such as telephone triage based estimation (Espino et al., 2003) and over the counter drug sales based estimation (Magruder, 2003).

The first web-based infectious disease surveillance was Google Flu Trends (GFT), which uses the Google query log dataset to predict the number of flu patients (Ginsberg et al., 2009). Although GFT has illustrated the effectiveness of web-based surveillance, the Google query log is not a public dataset.

Recent advances of the Web-based infectious disease surveillance depend mainly on open datasets such as those of Twitter (Zhang et al., 2017; Lampos et al., 2017; Iso et al., 2016; Wakamiya et al., 2016; Paul et al., 2014).

Zhang et al. (2017) use several indicator information resources and report the prediction performance obtained for the U.S., Italy, and Spain. Lampos et al. (2017) use word embedding (Mikolov et al., 2013) for enriching the feature selection of the flu model and thereby increase the inference performance. In Japan, the first successful system is that of Aramaki et al. (2011). They classify whether a user is infected by the flu or not for each tweet that includes a flu-related word. Wakamiya et al. (2016) examines the popularity difference between urban and rural cities for finer-grained infectious disease surveillance.

A state-of-the-art system for use with a Japanese infectious disease model by Iso et al. (2016) uses a time lag for improving nowcasting and for extending the forecasting model. However, they merely examine the prevalence rate throughout Japan; they do not consider the scale of user popularity.

This paper presents an examination of Twitter data through various scales of events, from infection of a few people to an epidemic affecting thousands of people, to detect Twitter-based detection performance.

3 Method

3.1 Extracting Tweets by Patients

To detect outbreaks of gastroenteritis with tweets, we estimate the number of patients.

First, the system collects Japanese tweets via Twitter API[1]. Then we select keyword sets of the following three typical patient complaints: *"nausea"*, *"chill"*, and *"diarrhea"*. This keyword sets are selected in preliminary experiments that use 11 major complaints (Chester et al., 2011). Using the tweet corpus collected in the previous step, we built a classifier that judges whether a given tweet is sent by a patient (positive) or not (negative). This task is a sentence binary classification. We used a SVM-based classifier under the bag-of-words (BOW) representation (Cortes and Vapnik, 1995; Joachims, 1998). Then we split a Japanese sentence into a sequence of words using a Japanese morphological analyzer, MeCab[2] (ver.0.98) with IPADic (ver.2.7.0) (Kudo et al., 2004). The polynomial kernel (d=2) is used as the kernel function. To build the training set, a human annotator assigned either a positive or negative label. For the labeling process, we followed conditions used in our previous study (Aramaki et al., 2011). Table 1 presents samples of tweets with labels.

Finally, we classified tweets into areas for area-based disease surveillance. The area is resolved based on metadata attached to a tweet as follows:

Table 1: Samples of labeled tweets

Tweet	keyword	P/N
When I got out of the bath I felt chilly. So I am wearing long sleeves and long pants, but now it's hot ('-'). I changed clothes ('-') It might be a cold ...	`chill`	P
I feel nauseous... I thought it resulted from coccyx pain, but I wonder. if I caught a cold.	`nausea`	P
I have diarrhea. I am going to a public restroom.	`diarrhea`	P
I really hate mantis. I hate them more than pigeons. I feel chilly when I think about it.	`chill`	N
whole-body exposure: 1 Gy nausea, Death year exposure is 10 Gy 1 ms	`nausea`	N
Meanwhile, Chiba prefecture announced on January 1 that 39 people that 39 people in Ichikawa City, Ibaraki prefecture, had group food poisoning complaining of symptoms such as diarrhea.	`diarrhea`	N

The tweet on the table are Japanese translations of English.

GPS Information: A tweet includes GPS data if a user allows the use of the location function. However, most users turn off this function for privacy reasons. Currently, the ratio of tweets with GPS information is only 0.46% (=35,635/7,666,201) in our dataset.

Profile Information: Several users include an address in a profile. We regard the user as near the profile address. The ratio of tweets with profile location is 26.2% (=2,010,605/7,666,201). To disambiguate the location names, we use a Geocoding service provided by Google Maps[3].

We removed the tweets without inferred geolocation for the study.

3.2 Linear Regression Analysis of Patient Numbers

Next we investigate the relation between the number of infected people and the number estimated using positive tweets. We use the number of infected people reported from the National Institute of Infectious Diseases (NIID) [4]. The number of infected people in each area is reported per sentinel weekly. To remove the population bias in areas, we calculate the **Incidence Rate (IR)** of people in an area during a week as follows.

$$IR_{repo}(a,t) = \frac{pat_{a,t}}{pop_a} \times 10^k \quad (1)$$

In that equation, $pat_{a,t}$ is the total number of all patients reported in the specified area a within the week index t, pop_a is the area's population, and k is a constant for correcting the value. In the experiment, k is set to 5.

[1] `https://dev.twitter.com/overview/api`

[2] `http://taku910.github.io/mecab/`

[3] `https://developers.google.com/maps/documentation/\geocoding/start`

[4] `https://www.niid.go.jp/niid/en/`

Then, we estimate the linear association between the IR_{repo} and the estimated one, IR_{est}, by application of multivariate linear regression as

$$IR_{est} = b_a^{s1} x_a^{s1} + b_a^{s2} x_a^{s2} + b_a^{s3} x_a^{s3} + b_p, \quad (2)$$

where x_a^s represents the number of positive tweets containing the specific word s. In addition, b_a^s and b_p are variables to be estimated.

4 Experiment

4.1 Setting

For this experiment, we estimated the Incidence Rate from positive tweets with the exploratory variables derived in Section 3.2. The experimental data consist of a training set and a test set. The data are shown in Table 2. For training, we used 1,720,325 tweets for 52 weeks from March 19, 2016 through December 31, 2016 for each area (47 areas in Japan).

Table 2: Dataset statistics

keyword	training	test
nausea	560,620 (53%)	594,443 (50%)
chill	378,652 (37%)	498,748 (35%)
diarrhea	781,053 (74%)	493,693 (69%)
Total	1,720,325 (34%)	1,586,884 (51%)

In brackets represents proportion of positive tweet

For clinical research, we estimated IR_{est} from the test set for 16 weeks from January 1, 2017 through April 19, 2017.

4.2 Results

The overall result is shown in Figure 2. Figure 3a and Figure 3b present details of results from two areas. Figure 3a presents a moderate example in *Nagano* area, where tweet-based estimation highly correlates with the reported values. In contrast, Figure 3b corresponding to *Tokyo* area reveals the weakness of our approach: the estimated value differs greatly from the reported value.

The difference between the two areas reflects the scale of the event. In Figure 3a, the reported values have one large peak (starting from 20 people to 30 people). In contrast, Figure 3b shows a slight increase in the reported values (from 13 to 15 during 15 weeks). From these results, the estimation of small events is difficult, causing numerous false-positive results.

5 Discussion

5.1 Event scale and Estimation Performance

Results reveal that Twitter-based estimation is often adversely affected by small events, yielding poor performance overall. However, in the case of large-scale events, the social sensor usually works well. For that reason, we investigated the relation between the (Sensor) Estimation Performance (EP) and the Event Scale (ES). For this work, we define these indicators as explained below.

Estimation Performance (EP): It is necessary to ascertain how accurately social sensors can estimate an event. We define this indicator as the correlation between IR_{repo} and IR_{est}.

Event Scale (ES): Fundamentally, the higher EP should be obtained when the epidemic scale (ES) is larger. We therefore assessed the correlation between the ES and the EP. We simply define ES based on the difference of IR in a time window as

$$ES = \max_{t \in T} IR(t) - \min_{t \in T} IR(t), \quad (3)$$

where T stands for a time window in the target timeline. $IR(t)$ is a function indicating IR at the week index t.

As for a time window, we divided the test set every 4 weeks (one window) and calculated IR. Correlation between EP and ES is shown in Figure 4. From Figure 4, correlation between EP and ES revealed poor performance (only 0.13). This result suggests that no overall correlation exists between EP and ES.

5.2 Discussion based on Epidemic Pattern

Not only the Event Scale (ES) but also event pattern would affect EP. We considered that event pattern classified by epidemic phase, such as the beginning and the end:

Increasing ↗ is the phase of the beginning of the epidemic during which the IR increases during the target time window.

Decreasing ↘ is the phase of the end of the epidemic during which the IR decreases during the target time window.

Peak $\wedge$ is the phase of the epidemic peak during which the maximum of the IR is observed.

Between $\vee$ is intermediate of two epidemic peaks.

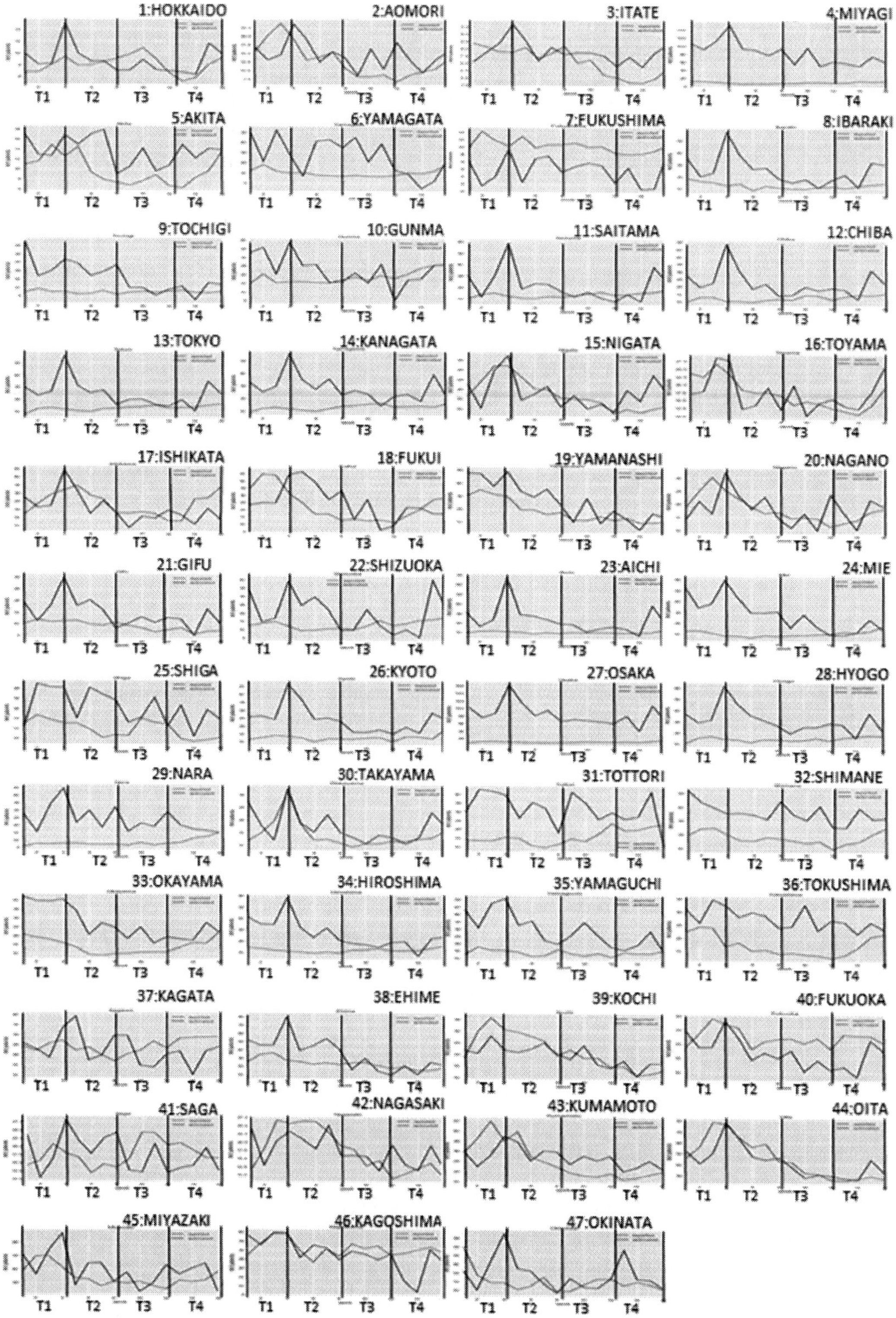

Figure 2: Result for each area. The X-axis indicates the time line (week). The Y-axis indicates the Incidence Rate (IR). *T* indicates the time window (4 weeks).

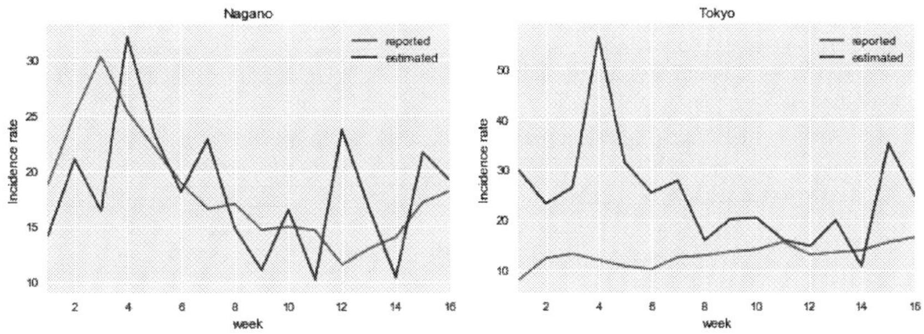

(a) Example: Nagano

(b) Example: Tokyo

Figure 3: Representative results in two areas: (a) Nagano and (b) Tokyo. The red line shows IR_{repo}. The blue one shows IR_{est}.

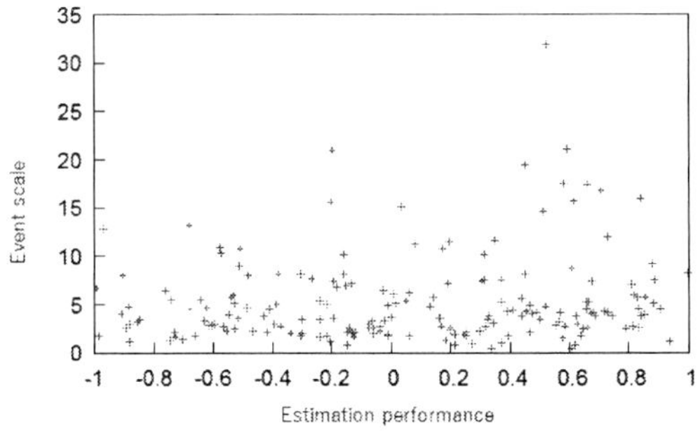

Figure 4: Relation between EP (X-axis) and ES (Y-axis). This revealed poor performance ($r = 0.13$).

The detailed definition is presented in Table 3. The table presents a window for which $IR_b - IR_i > 0$ and $IR_b - IR_e > 0$ (represented as $IR_b - IR_i > 0$ and $IR_b - IR_e > 0$) is regarded as the *increasing* Pattern.

The results are presented in Table 4, indicating correlation between the EP and ES for each Pattern. As the table shows, the performance showed divergence in each Pattern. For instance, the *decreasing* Pattern showed high correlation ($r = 0.305$). In contrast, the *between* Pattern shows quite poor performance (less than 0 correlation).

5.3 Discussion based on Area Population

The number of tweets is related to the population Therefore, we inferred that the EP is affected by the population of each area. We classified each window by four types based on population. We defined the four types as explained below.

Super High population area (SHP) is area with population of 2.5 million or more

High population area (HP) is area with population of 1.5 million to 2.5 million

Low population area (LP) is area with population of 1 million to 1.5 million

Super Low population area (SLP) is area with population of 1 million or less

Table 5 shows the correlation between the EP and ES in each population area. From Table 5, in high population area (1.5 million to 2.5 million), weak correlation was found ($r = 0.214$). Furthermore, correlation between EP and ES is related to population.

5.4 Combination of Factors

As described above, we introduced three factors that affected the estimation performance (EP): (1) event scale (ES), (2) event pattern, and (3) area population. In this section, we combined the above findings, and investigated the correlation coefficient between the performance and the (1) ES in each factor, (2) event pattern (four types) and (3) area population (four types). The 16 obtained combinations are shown in Table 6.

From Table 6, when the epidemic decreases greatly in areas with low population, the performance tends to be high. Especially, this trend is significant for *decreasing* pattern in low and super low population areas. In contrast, *peak* and *between* pattern show poor correlation.

From practical viewpoints, the *increasing* pattern is important because catching the increase or decrease of patients contributes to prevention. Figure 5 presents the relation between the EP and ES in *increasing* pattern in the high population area, which shows moderate correlation ($r = 0.378$). In

Table 3: Patterns of Epidemic Phase. Each pattern is classified by three phase: IR_b, IR_i and IR_e. The IR_b is the IR at the beginning of the target window. The IR_i is the average IR of all weeks, except for the beginning and the end. In the experiments, the window size is 4 weeks. Consequently, the IR_i is the average IR of the second and third weeks. The IR_e is the IR at the end of the target window.

Pattern	$IR_b - IR_i$	$IR_b - IR_e$	of samples
Increasing ↗	+	+	55
Decreasing ↘	−	−	45
Peak ∧	+	−	56
Between ∨	−	+	32

Table 4: Correlation between EP and ES in each pattern

Pattern	correlation
Increasing ↗	0.098
Decreasing ↘	0.305
Peak ∧	-0.024
Between ∨	0.058

Table 5: Correlation between EP and ES in each area population

Population	correlation
SHP area	0.125
HP area	0.214
LP area	0.185
SLP area	0.059

the figure, moderate performance ($r > 0.8$ in the X-axis) is obtained when the ES is greater than 7 in the Y-axis. It corresponds to a greater than 150 patient increase in a month.

From this result, we can estimate the borderline of the reliable warning that is 150 patient increasing or decreasing in the high population area.

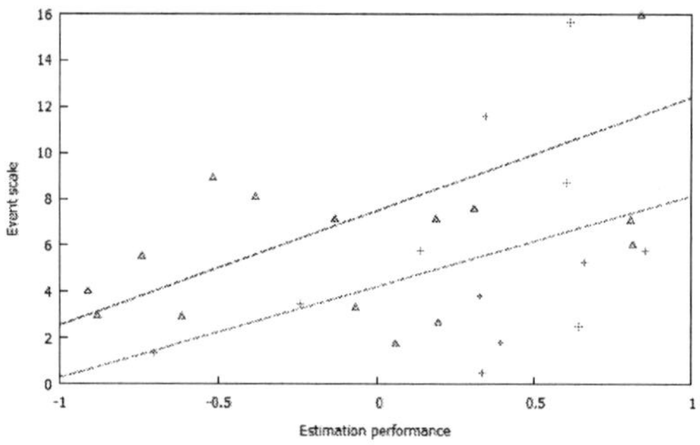

Figure 5: Relation between EP (X-axis) and ES (Y-axis) in the Increasing Pattern in the High Population area (plot with blue triangle) and the Decreasing Pattern in the Low Population area (plot with red cross). This situation for which performance depends on the scale.

Table 6: Correlation between EP and ES in the combination of event pattern and population areas

	SHP area	HP area	LP area	SLP area
Increasing ↗	0.255	0.378	0.01	-0.112
Decreasing ↘	-0.678	0.164	**0.550****	**0.538***
Peak ∧	0.144	0.063	-0.394	0.411
Between ∨	0.494	0.411	-0.409	0.179

Bold font indicates significant correlation (** is $p < 0.05$, * is $p < 0.10$).

5.5 Practical Contribution and Future Direction

To date, social sensors have demonstrated their potential feasibility for various event detections. However, the practical application is rarely launched. One reason is the lack of reliability of social sensors. In other words, we can never fully trust social sensor-based information.

Results of this study demonstrated that the event scale and the estimation performance of social sensor are related. We think this finding is practically important because this characteristic provides important information for the following two use cases:

1. In cases where a really big epidemic occurs, we can believe that the system must detect the clue of the epidemic.

2. In contrast, in cases where the system estimation is normal, we can at least infer that the current situation is not crisis.

From a practical viewpoint, these features that can engage such safety are important. Based on these results, we are developing a surveillance service supported by Infectious Disease Surveillance Center (IDSC). In the near future, we would like to report a case of a system-running experience.

This report describes our attempt at the detection of small and unseasonal disease events.

The method employs the regression of disease-related word frequencies. Results of the experiment, based on Japanese 47 areas from January 2017 to April 2017, suggests that the detection of small events is difficult (r = 0.13). Although the overall performance is poor, the event scale (change in the number of patients) and the detection performance size show correlation (the phase of epidemic in high population area shows a correlation ratio of $r = 0.38$). We think this finding is practically important because it enables realization of a practical system that is useful in the following two use cases. (1) If a truly large epidemic occurs, we can infer that the system must detect it, (2) In other words, the system estimation is low, we can at least infer that the current situation is not so severe. These characteristics are fundamentally important for use in protecting public safety.

In future work, we plan to apply other classification algorithms and compare the performance. Furthermore, we will examine the indicator to represent the ES more effectively.

Acknowledgements

This work was supported by Japan Agency for Medical Research and Development (Grant Number: 16768699) and JST ACT-I.

References

Eiji Aramaki, Sachiko Maskawa, and Mizuki Morita. 2011. Twitter catches the flu: Detecting influenza epidemics using twitter. In Proc. of EMNLP. pp. 1568–1576.

Tammy L Stuart Chester, Marsha Taylor, Jat Sandhu, Sara Forsting, Andrea Ellis, Rob Stirling, and Eleni Galanis. 2011. Use of a web forum and an online questionnaire in the detection and investigation of an outbreak. Online Journal of Public Health Informatics 3(1).

Corinna Cortes and Vladimir Vapnik. 1995. Support-vector networks. Machine Learning 20(3):273–297.

Aron Culotta. 2013. Lightweight methods to estimate influenza rates and alcohol sales volume from twitter messages. Lang. Resour. Eval. 47(1):217–238.

Ernesto Diaz-Aviles and Avaré Stewart. 2012. Tracking twitter for epidemic intelligence: Case study: Ehec/hus outbreak in germany, 2011. In Proc. of WebSci. pp. 82–85.

J. Espino, W. Hogan, and M. Wagner. 2003. Telephone triage: A timely data source for surveillance of influenza-like diseases. In Proc. of AMIA Annual Symposium. pp. 215–219.

Jeremy Ginsberg, Matthew H Mohebbi, Rajan S Patel, Lynnette Brammer, Mark S Smolinski, and Larry Brilliant. 2009. Detecting influenza epidemics using search engine query data. Nature 457(7232):1012–1014.

Hayate Iso, Shoko Wakamiya, and Eiji Aramaki. 2016. Forecasting word model: Twitter-based influenza surveillance and prediction. In Proc. of COLING. pp. 76–86.

Thorsten Joachims. 1998. Text categorization with support vector machines: Learning with many relevant features. In proc. of ECML pp. 137–142.

Taku Kudo, Kaoru Yamamoto, and Yuji Matsumoto. 2004. Applying conditional random fields to japanese morphological analysis. In Proc. of EMNLP. volume 4, pp. 230–237.

Vasileios Lampos and Nello Cristianini. 2010. Tracking the flu pandemic by monitoring the social web. In Proc. of CIP. pp. 411–416.

Vasileios Lampos, Andrew C Miller, Steve Crossan, and Christian Stefansen. 2015. Advances in nowcasting influenza-like illness rates using search query logs. Scientific Reports 5.

Vasileios Lampos, Bin Zou, and Ingemar Johansson Cox. 2017. Enhancing feature selection using word embeddings: The case of flu surveillance. In Proc. of WWW. International World Wide Web Conferences Steering Committee, Republic and Canton of Geneva, Switzerland, pp. 695–704.

S. Magruder. 2003. Evaluation of over-the-counter pharmaceutical sales as a possible early warning indicator of human disease. In Johns Hopkins University APL Technical Digest (24).

Tomas Mikolov, Ilya Sutskever, Kai Chen, Greg S Corrado, and Jeff Dean. 2013. Distributed representations of words and phrases and their compositionality. In Proc. of NIRS. pp. 3111–3119.

Michael J Paul, Mark Dredze, and David Broniatowski. 2014. Twitter improves influenza forecasting. PLoS Currents Outbreaks .

Takeshi Sakaki, Makoto Okazaki, and Yutaka Matsuo. 2010. Earthquake shakes twitter users: Real-time event detection by social sensors. In Proc. of WWW. pp. 851–860.

Shoko Wakamiya, Yukiko Kawai, and Eiji Aramaki. 2016. After the boom no one tweets: microblog-based influenza detection incorporating indirect information. In Proc. of EDB. pp. 17–25.

Qian Zhang, Nicola Perra, Daniela Perrotta, Michele Tizzoni, Daniela Paolotti, and Alessandro Vespignani. 2017. Forecasting seasonal influenza fusing digital indicators and a mechanistic disease model. In Proc. of WWW. pp. 311–319.

Incorporating Dependency Trees Improve Identification of Pregnant Women on Social Media Platforms

Yi-Jie Huang[1], Chu Hsien Su[2], Yi-Chun Chang[3], Tseng-Hsin Ting[3], Tzu-Yuan Fu[3], Rou-Min Wang[3], Hong-Jie Dai[3*], Yung-Chun Chang[4*], Jitendra Jonnagaddala[5] and Wen-Lian Hsu[6]

[1]Department of Computer Science, National Tsing Hua University, Hsinchu, Taiwan.
[2]Department of Psychiatry, National Taiwan University Hospital, Taipei, Taiwan.
[3]Department of Computer Science and Information Engineering, National Taitung University, Taitung, Taiwan.
[4]Graduate Institute of Data Science, Taipei Medical University, Taipei, Taiwan.
[5]School of Public Health and Community Medicine, University of New South Wales, Sydney, Australia.
[6]Institute of Information Science, Academia Sinica, Taipei, Taiwan.

Abstract

The increasing popularity of social media lead users to share enormous information on the internet. This information has various application like, it can be used to develop models to understand or predict user behavior on social media platforms. For example, few online retailers have studied the shopping patterns to predict shopper's pregnancy stage. Another interesting application is to use the social media platforms to analyze users' health-related information. In this study, we developed a tree kernel-based model to classify tweets conveying pregnancy related information using this corpus. The developed pregnancy classification model achieved an accuracy of 0.847 and an F-score of 0.565. A new corpus from popular social media platform Twitter was developed for the purpose of this study. In future, we would like to improve this corpus by reducing noise such as retweets.

1 Introduction

The web has become a powerful medium for disseminating information about diverse topics, people can share information anytime and anywhere. Real-time user generated information on the web, epitomized by social media and in particular microblogs, are becoming an important data source to complement existing resources for disease surveillance (Brownstein, Freifeld, & Madoff, 2009), behavioral medicine (Ayers, Althouse, & Dredze, 2014), and public health (Dredze, 2012). Studies have shown that 26% of online adults discuss health information using social media(GE-Healthcare, 2012), with approximately 90% women using online media for health-care information, and 60% using pregnancy related apps for support. These statistics suggest that social media sources may contain key information regarding specific cohorts, such as pregnant women, and their drug usage habits. Twitter—a micro-blogging site which is actively used by over 328 million users[1]—is a very popular social network currently being extensively used for public health monitoring tasks (Chandrashekar, Magge, Sarker, & Gonzalez, 2017; Jonnagaddala, Jue, & Dai). It is also an attractive resource for biosurveillance related shared tasks and competitions because it carries health-related knowledge expressed by various cohorts(Adam, Jonnagaddala, Chughtai, & Macintyre, 2017). However, the noisy nature of data on Twitter demands sophisticated models and techniques for mining the knowledge encapsulated.

The primary aim of this study is to detect whether a tweet convey pregnancy or not. This information further downstream can be used to study the safety of drugs in pregnancy are of paramount importance. Typically, pregnant woman in social media are detected using simple regular expressions and rules such as – matching the phrase

* Corresponding author

[1] https://about.twitter.com/company

Proceedings of the International Workshop on Digital Disease Detection using Social Media 2017 (DDDSM-2017), pages 26–32, Taipei, Taiwan, November 27, 2017. ©2017 AFNLP *"i am twenty weeks pregnant"* (Chandrashekar et al., 2017; Wang, Paul, & Dredze, 2014). However, employing rule based detection can lead to many false positives since it doesn't consider context or sentiment embedded in the tweet. Often, the tweets recognised by rule based methods seem to be sarcastic. For example, consider the tweet *"I look like I'm 6 months pregnant"*. This tweet is a sarcastic tweet and the user actually is not pregnant. Thus, in order to overcome this issue, we propose to use a tree kernel-based approach to detect pregnant woman more effectively. Tree kernel-based approaches have been applied to many different researches, such as relation extraction (Culotta and Sorensen, 2004), question classification (Zhang and Lee, 2003) and protein interaction detection (Miwa et al., 2010). In recent years, tree kernel-based models were used to analyze Twitter data, but most of those studies were focused on opinion mining and sentiment classification (Agarwal et al., 2011; Alicante et al., 2016). In this study, we investigate the effectiveness of applying the approach on the task of determining whether a tweet is posted by a pregnant woman or not.

2 Related Work

Most of the studies in mining Twitter are focused on drug safety domain, e.g. drug abuse and adverse drug reaction (Dai, Touray, Wang, Jonnagaddala, & Syed-Abdul, 2016; Sarker et al., 2016). However, this information can also be used for health surveillance of pregnant women. The study most related to ours is presented by (Chandrashekar et al., 2017) in which they annotated 1,200 tweets with pregnancy announcements to allow the identification of pregnancy trimesters. Klein et. al, constructed an annotated corpus from Twitter focusing on personal medication intake (Klein, Sarker, Rouhizadeh, O'Connor, & Gonzalez, 2017). In an another related study an integrated corpus composing of 2,000 sentences from Twitter and PubMed called TwiMed was presented (Alvaro, Miyao, & Collier, 2017). The corpus contains the annotations of diseases, symptoms and drugs, and their relations.

Tree kernel-based approaches have been widely applied to text classification tasks. Zhang and Lee (2003) utilized tree kernel to question classification and demonstrated that syntactic structures is useful for questions classification. However, the space of tree fragments is too large to compute their inner products. In order to recursively and efficiently compute the common substructures similarity between two trees, Moschitti (2006) proposed convolution tree kernel and developed a toolkit for public. Wang et al. (2009) adopted convolution tree kernel to find out similar questions from Yahoo Answers dataset. They observed that the convolution tree kernel function can effectively utilize the syntactic structure of a sentence. On the other hand, Agarwal (2011) applied partial tree kernel (PTK) to classify sentiment polarity of twitter data and achieved remarkable performance. The kernel provides the ability to analyze additional semantic information by considering the contribution of shared subsequences containing all children of nodes. PTK compares words by the order of alphabets to determine word similarity for ameliorating the weak point of convolution tree kernel. Later on Croce et al. (2011) proposed smoothing partial tree kernel (SPTK) and improved the calculation method of word similarity by using singular value decomposition (SVD) to transform all words into vectors for determining the cosine similarity between them.

In this paper, we built models based on SPTK and three kinds of tree structures. Besides part-of-speech (POS) tags, the new tree structures incorporate dependency tree and grammatical relations for extracting more useful features. Furthermore, we used word embedding to substitute the vectors generated by SVD. Many studies have demonstrated that word embedding is really useful in many natural language processing tasks. With this in mind we also investigated the effectiveness of combining word embedding with SPTK and different tree structures on the task of identifying pregnancy women on Twitter.

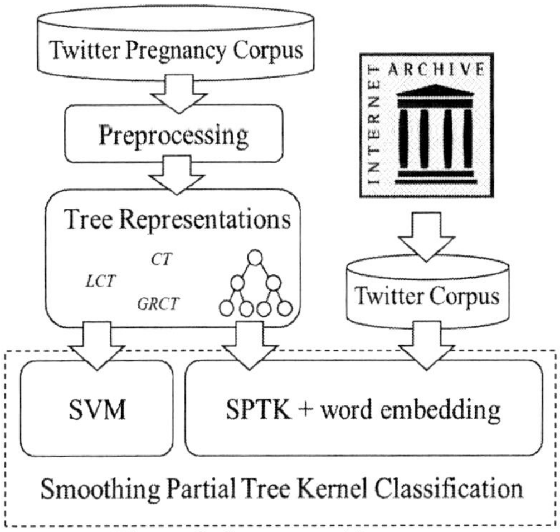

Figure 1: System architecture

3 Methods

The Figure 1 shows the architecture of the proposed pregnancy detection method. The architecture comprises three key components: preprocessing, tree representations, and smoothing partial tree kernel classification. Firstly, the preprocessing component processes a set of tweets that may convey pregnancy (called *candidate tweets* hereafter) through heuristic rules. Then, each candidate tweet is represented by three kinds of tree structures for capturing the information of syntactic, content, and semantic of the tweet. Finally, the smoothing partial tree-kernel classification component measures the similarity between tweet in terms of their tree structures, and the tree kernel is incorporated into support vector machine (SVM) for learning a classifier. We elaborate each component in the following sub-sections.

3.1 Preprocessing

Given a tweet, we first apply the Stanford parser[2] to generate the output of parse tree and PoS tagging. We further remove stop words and URLs from tweets. In addition, we observe that retweet is impossible to convey pregnancy since Twitter's retweet feature is to help users quickly share that tweet with all of users' followers. Therefore, we filter out tweets if the text start with "RT" (i.e. retweet). By filtering out retweets, the rest are the candidate tweets which may convey pregnancy.

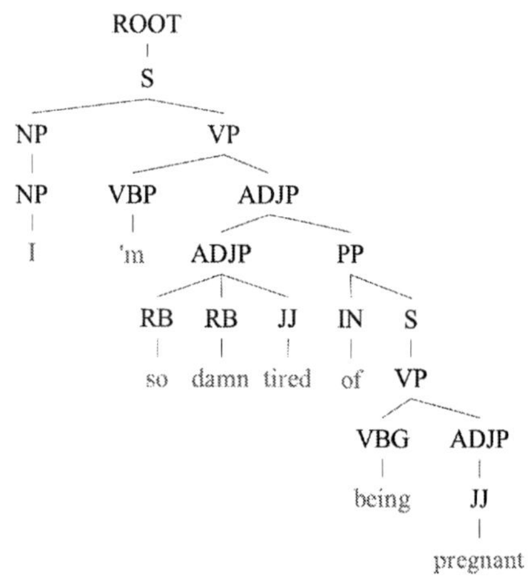

Figure 2: Constituency tree (CT)

3.2 Tree Representations

Different tree representations in tree kernel-based approach may lead to modeling more effective syntactic or semantic feature spaces. In this paper, three kinds tree structure are used to represent tweet, they are constituency tree (CT), lexical centered tree (LCT), and grammatical relation centered tree (GRCT). To facilitate comprehension of the different tree representations, we take a pregnant woman's Tweet "*I'm so damn tired of being pregnant*" as an example.

Figure 2 is CT, which is the basic tree representation generated by Stanford Parser. The parser works out the grammatical structure of sentences by grouping words together as phrases that could represent the subject or object of a verb. However, CT only contain information of the grammatical structure. Croce et al. (2011) proposed GRCT and LCT to complement CT. GRCT and LCT involve grammatical relations (GR), PoS tags and dependencies. GRCT adds tags of grammatical relations and lexical information as new nodes in CT to emphasize grammatical relationship information while LCT enhance the lexical information by adding grammatical relations and PoS-tags as the rightmost children. Figure 3 and Figure 4 show the same example sentence for GRCT and LCT.

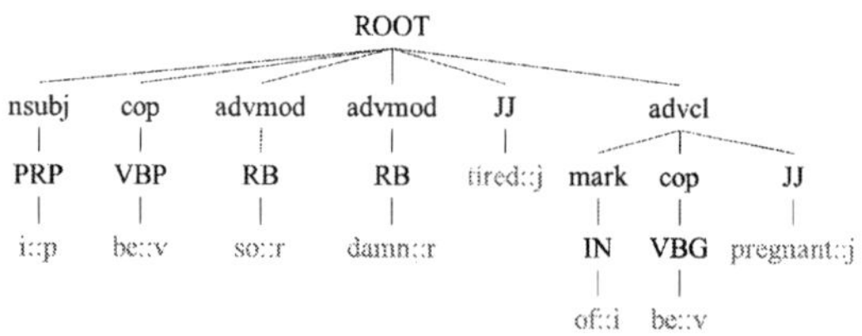

Figure 3: Grammatical relation centered tree (GRCT)

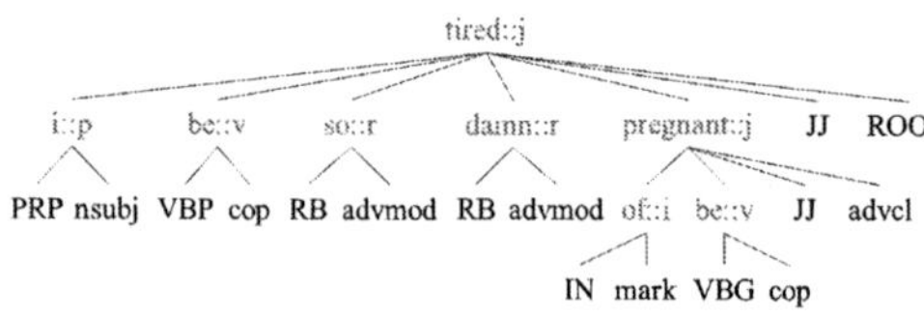

Figure 4: Lexical centered tree (LCT)

3.3 Smoothing Partial Tree Kernel Classification

In SVMs, a kernel function is employed to cleverly compute the similarity between two instances

[2] http://nlp.stanford.edu/software/lex-parser.shtml

without requiring the identification of the entire feature space. In the case of tree kernel, it represents tree in terms of their substructures and evaluates the number of common tree fragments between two trees T_1 and T_2 through the following equation:

$$K(T_1,T_2) = \sum_{n_1 \in N_{T_1}} \sum_{n_2 \in N_{T_2}} \Delta(n_1,n_2) \quad (1)$$

where N_{T_1} and N_{T_2} denote the sets of nodes in T_1 and T_2, respectively. The function $\Delta(n_1, n_2)$ is equal to the number of common fragments rooted in the n_1 and n_2 nodes. Since the number of different sub-trees is exponential with the parse tree size, it is computationally infeasible to directly use the feature vector.

In recent years, multiple tree kernels have been proposed for resolving this computation issue, such as syntactic tree kernel (Collins and Duffy, 2002), partial tree kernel (Moschitti, 2006), and lexical semantic kernel (Basili et al., 2005). However, the lexical in these tree kernels must belong to the leaf nodes of exactly the same structures limits its applications. Trivially, it cannot work on dependency trees. Croce et al. (2011) proposed a much more general smoothed tree kernel (i.e. smoothing partial tree kernel, SPTK) that can be applied to any tree and exploit any combination of lexical similarities, respecting the syntax enforced by the tree. Therefore, we adopt SPTK to capture the syntactic similarity between the above high dimensional vectors implicitly, as well as partial lexical similarity of trees. The $\Delta_{SPTK}(n_1, n_2)$ can be defined as follows:

(1) If nodes n_1 and n_2 are leaves, then $\Delta_{SPTK}(n_1, n_2) = \mu\lambda\sigma(n_1, n_2)$
(2) Otherwise, calculate $\Delta_{SPTK}(n_1, n_2)$ recursively as:

$$\Delta_\sigma(n_1,n_2) = \mu\sigma(n_1,n_2)\times(\lambda^2 + \sum_{\vec{I}_1,\vec{I}_2,l(\vec{I}_1)=l(\vec{I}_2)} \lambda^{d(\vec{I}_1)+d(\vec{I}_2)} \times \prod_{j=1}^{l(\vec{I}_1)} \Delta_\sigma(c_{n1}(\vec{I}_{1j}),c_{n2}(\vec{I}_{2j}))), \quad (2)$$

where σ is any similarity between nodes, μ, $\lambda \in [0,1]$ are two decay factors, $\vec{I}_1$ and $\vec{I}_2$ are two sequence of indices, which index subsequences of children u, $\vec{I} = (i_1,...,i_{|u|})$, in sequences of children s, $1 \le i_1 < ... < i_{|u|} \le |s|$, i.e., such that $u = s_{i1}...s_{i|u|}$, and $d(\vec{I}) = i_{|u|} - i_1 + 1$ is the distance between the first and last child. c is one of the children of the node n, also in indexed by $\vec{I}$. This provides an advantage that tree fragments can be matched by applying word embedding similarity σ. Even those tree fragments are not identical but are semantically related.

3.4 Dataset

To the best of our knowledge, there is no openly available corpus for pregnant woman detection. Therefore, we compiled a dataset for the performance evaluation. We employed Tweetinvi[3] to collect tweets mentioning pregnancy written in English from May 1, 2017 to May 29, 2017. To retrieve the tweets, we used a list of pregnancy-related query terms to search tweets online. For all 14,824 collected raw tweets, we pre-processed them by removing emoticons, line feeds, extra spaces and dots based on regular expression. The collected tweets contain duplications owing to the same tweets retrieved by different queries and the retweets shared by different users. We removed duplicated tweets or tweets contain similar descriptions by calculating Levenshtein distance among the collected tweets. If the similarity score of two tweets is larger than 70%, we discard the shorter one and reserve the longer one. Finally, we obtained 7,984 tweet sentences.

We randomly selected 3,000 tweets from the collected dataset to build an initial corpus. Five annotators were recruited to annotate the corpus by using MAE (Multi-document Annotation Environment) (Rim, 2016). They determined whether the tweet authors are pregnant or not based on the context information and gave "Yes" or "No" annotations indicating positive or negative cases. A preliminary consistency test was conducted on 500 tweets by having the first two of the annotators annotate the data, while the last one checked their annotations for consistency. The Fleiss' kappa coefficient value for the initial consistency test is 0.42 (moderate agreements). After examining the consistency, all annotators adjusted their annotations and re-annotated the entire data set. After finishing the annotation process, a voting method was employed to determine the

[3] https://github.com/linvi/tweetinvi

final annotation for each tweet resulting in a corpus containing 642 positive and 2,358 negative annotations.

3.5 Experimental Setting

We use the KeLP package (Simone Filice, 2015) to implement SPTK classification component, and develop three kinds tree representations. To derive credible evaluation results, we utilize the 10-folds cross validation method (Manning and Schütze, 1999). The evaluation metrics used to determine relative effectiveness of the compared methods include the precision, recall, F_1-score, and accuracy (Manning and Schütze, 1999).

For computing lexical similarity, we collected approximating 15.8M tweets from Internet Archive[4] instead of using existing pre-trained word embeddings. In the collected dataset, we removed non-English tweets and transformed each word to its lemma for learning word embeddings (300-dimension) through continuous bag of words with default settings of the word2vec[5] toolkit (Mikolov et al., 2013).

4. Results and Discussion

The performance comparison of our methods with other methods is provided in the Table 1. In order to show complexity of pregnancy detection, the convolution tree kernel with constituency tree (TK_{CT}) was used as the baseline method. We also compared the performance with other two tree structures that included grammatical functions and dependency (TK_{GRCT} and TK_{LCT}) respectively. Moreover, smoothing partial tree kernel with both dependency tree structures were also compared ($SPTK_{GRCT}$ and $SPTK_{LCT}$).

Method	*P.*	*R.*	*F₁*	*Acc.*
TK_{CT}	**74.61**	37.60	50.00	83.90
TK_{GRCT}	63.90	40.81	49.81	82.40
TK_{LCT}	70.82	44.24	54.46	84.17
$SPTK_{GRCT}$	65.50	40.81	50.29	82.73
$SPTK_{LCT}$	71.88	**46.57**	**56.52**	**84.67**

Table 1: The pregnant woman recognition results of compared methods.

As shown in Table 1, the TK_{CT} with the basic tree kernel method can only achieve a mediocre performance. On the contrary, since GRCT and LCT encode the dependency information and grammatical relation in the tree structures, using both dependency tree can benefit the performance of pregnancy detection. It is worth mentioning that TK_{LCT} outperforms TK_{GRCT}, this indicates utilizing lexical features as central node is effective in representing pregnancy information in a tweet. Finally, the SPTK considers lexical similarities on the tree structure to extract features of pregnant woman posts. Therefore, $SPTK_{LCT}$ achieves the best detection performance with an F_1-score of 56.52%.

Figure 5 illustrates a word cloud consisting of the top 100 words frequently occurring in the positive and negative tweets of the corpus. The pink words refer to the positive ones and the blue refer to the negative ones. We excluded mention tags (e.g. @John), numeric numbers, punctuations, and words listed in the stop word list[6]. We observed that among the top 100 words, 55% of them appeared in both positive and negative cases. We also checked the words that are only included in the positive and negative word frequency, and we did not find anything special except the positive words "father" and "husband" and negative word "abortion". It seems that the use of words between positive and negative corpus are highly consistent. The reasons caused this condition we thought that we used the simple and similar queries to search twitter and the negative corpus is larger than the positive corpus.

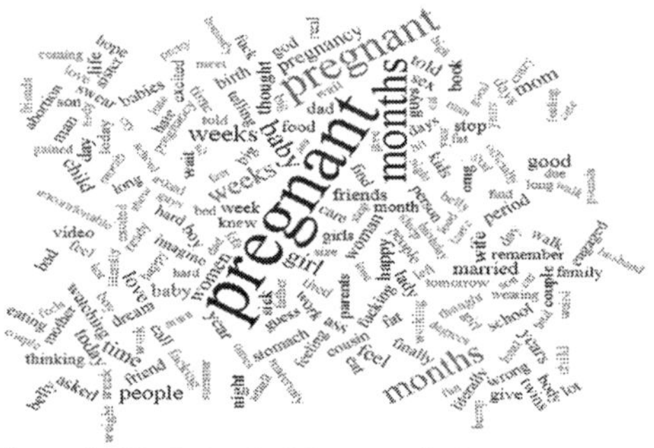

Figure 5: Word cloud of the compiled corpus. Colors and their corresponding category: Pink – Positive and Blue - Negative.

5 Conclusion

We presented a tree kernel-based model to identify tweets posted by pregnant women. Unlike traditional approaches which detect using regular expression patterns or rules, we employ different tree

[4] A non-profit library of millions of free books, movies, software, music, websites.

[5] https://code.google.com/archive/p/word2vec/

[6] http://www.webconfs.com/stop-words.php

structures together with two tree kernels that incorporate the dependency and grammatical relation information represented in the form of tree structures. We evaluated our models on manually annotated Twitter corpus specifically developed for the purpose of this study. The results demonstrate that employing dependency tree can improve the performance of pregnancy detection. We also observe that lexical features as central node is effective in representing pregnancy information in a tweet. The best performed model had an F-score of 0.5652 on our corpus. The SPTK model considers lexical similarities on the tree structure.

In future, we would like to explore different ways to integrate deeper semantics into tree structure for pregnancy detection on social media platforms. Moreover, we also would like to improve the corpus by ignoring retweets, avoid possible noise and obtain more meta data such as timestamp details. In addition, the pregnancy related tweets may reveal the other health behaviour related information of the of the pregnant authors like drug usage, food intake, any disease symptoms, and emotion. We would like to use this information in future to conduct syndromic surveillance on pregnant women using social media.

Acknowledgments

We are grateful for the constructive comments from three anonymous reviewers. This work was supported by grant MOST106-3114-E-001- 002 and MOST105-2221-E-001-008-MY3 from the Ministry of Science and Technology, Taiwan.

Reference

Alfred. V. Aho and Jeffrey D. Ullman. 1972. The Theory of Parsing, Translation and Compiling, volume 1. Prentice-Hall, Englewood Cliffs, NJ.

American Psychological Association. 1983. Publications Manual. American Psychological Association, Washington, DC.

Ashok K. Chandra, Dexter C. Kozen, and Larry J. Stockmeyer. 1981. Alternation. Journal of the Association for Computing Machinery, 28(1):114-133.

Association for Computing Machinery. 1983. Computing Reviews, 24(11):503-512.

Dan Gusfield. 1997. Algorithms on Strings, Trees and Sequences. Cambridge University Press, Cambridge, UK.

Adam, D., Jonnagaddala, J., Chughtai, A. A., & Macintyre, C. R. (2017). *ZikaHack 2016: A digital disease detection competition.* Paper presented at the Proceedings of the International Workshop on Digital Disease Detection using Social Media 2017, Taipei, Taiwan.

Alvaro, N., Miyao, Y., & Collier, N. (2017). TwiMed: Twitter and PubMed Comparable Corpus of Drugs, Diseases, Symptoms, and Their Relations. *JMIR Public Health and Surveillance, 3*(2).

Ayers, J. W., Althouse, B. M., & Dredze, M. (2014). Could behavioral medicine lead the web data revolution? *Jama, 311*(14), 1399-1400.

Brownstein, J. S., Freifeld, C. C., & Madoff, L. C. (2009). Digital disease detection—harnessing the Web for public health surveillance. *New England Journal of Medicine, 360*(21), 2153-2157.

Chandrashekar, P. B., Magge, A., Sarker, A., & Gonzalez, G. (2017). Social media mining for identification and exploration of health-related information from pregnant women. *arXiv preprint arXiv:1702.02261.*

Dai, H.-J., Touray, M., Wang, C.-K., Jonnagaddala, J., & Syed-Abdul, S. (2016). Feature Engineering for Recognizing Adverse Drug Reactions from Twitter Posts. *Information.*

Dredze, M. (2012). How social media will change public health. *IEEE Intelligent Systems, 27*(4), 81-84.

GE-Healthcare. (2012). Twenty six percent of online adults discuss health information online; privacy cited as the biggest barrier to entry. Retrieved from http://www.businesswire.com/news/home/20121120005872/en/Twenty-percent-online-adults-discuss-health-information

Jonnagaddala, J., Jue, T. R., & Dai, H. *Binary classification of Twitter posts for adverse drug reactions.*

Klein, A. Z., Sarker, A., Rouhizadeh, M., O'Connor, K., & Gonzalez, G. (2017). Detecting Personal Medication Intake in Twitter: An Annotated Corpus and Baseline Classification System. *BioNLP 2017*, 136.

Rim, K. (2016). *MAE2: Portable Annotation Tool for General Natural Language Use.* Paper presented at the In Proceedings of the 12th Joint ACL-ISO Workshop on Interoperable Semantic Annotation, Portorož, Slovenia, May 28, 2016.

Sarker, A., O'Connor, K., Ginn, R., Scotch, M., Smith, K., Malone, D., & Gonzalez, G. (2016). Social Media Mining for Toxicovigilance: Automatic Monitoring of Prescription Medication Abuse from Twitter. *Drug Safety, 39*(3), 231-240. doi:10.1007/s40264-015-0379-4

Wang, S., Paul, M. J., & Dredze, M. (2014). *Exploring health topics in Chinese social media: An analysis of Sina Weibo.* Paper presented at the

AAAI Workshop on the World Wide Web and Public Health Intelligence.

Simone Filice, Giuseppe Castellucci, Danilo Croce and Roberto Basili. 2015. KeLP: a Kernel-based Learning Platform for Natural Language Processing. *Proceedings of ACL-IJCNLP 2015 System Demonstrations*, pages 19–24.

Michael Collins and Nigel Duffy. 2002. New Ranking Algorithms for Parsing and Tagging: Kernels over Discrete Structures, and the Voted Perceptron. In *Proceedings of ACL'02.*

Danilo Croce, Alessandro Moschitti and Robert Basili. 2011. Structured lexical similarity via convolution kernels on dependency trees. In *Proceedings of the 2011 Conference on Empirical Methods in Natural Language Processing (EMNLP)*, pp. 1034–1046, Edinburgh, UK.

Alessandro Moschitti. 2004. A Study on Convolution Kernels for Shallow Semantic Parsing. In *Proceedings of the 42nd Annual Meeting on Association for Computational Linguistics.* Association for Computational Linguistics, Stroudsburg, PA, USA, ACL'04.

Thorsten Joachims. 1999. Making Large-scale Support Vector Machine Learning Practical. In Bernhard Schölkopf, Christopher J. C. Burges, and Alexander J. Smola, editors, *Advances in Kernel Methods*, MIT Press, Cambridge, MA, USA, pages 169–184. http://dl.acm.org/citation.cfm?id=299094.299104.

Aron Culotta and Jeffrey Sorensen. 2004. Dependency tree kernels for relation extraction. In *Proceedings of ACL'04.*

Dell Zhang and Wee Sun Lee. 2003. Question classification using support vector machines. In *Proceedings of the 26th Annual International ACM SIGIR Conference on Research and Development in Informaion Retrieval*, New York, NY, pp. 26–32. ACM Press

Makoto Miwa, Rune Sætre, Yusuke Miyao and Jun'ichi Tsujii. 2009. Protein-protein interaction extraction by leveraging multiple kernels and parsers. *International Journal of Medical Informatics*, 78(12):e39–e46.

Apoorv Agarwal, Boyi Xie, Ilia Vovsha, Owen Rambow and Rebecca Passonneau. 2011. Sentiment analysis of twitter data. In: *Proceedings of ACL'11 Workshop on Languages in Social Media*. pp. 30–38.

Anita Alicante, Anna Corazza and Antonio Piront. 2016. In *Proceedings of Third Italian Conference on Computational Linguistics (CLiC-it 2016) & Fifth Evaluation Campaign of Natural Language Processing and Speech Tools for Italian. Final Workshop (EVALITA 2016).*

Tomas Mikolov, Kai Chen, Greg Corrado, and Jeffrey Dean. 2013. Efficient estimation of word representations in vector space. In *Proceedings of ICLR'13 Workshop*.

Christopher D. Manning and Hinrich Schütze. 1999. Foundations of statistical natural language processing. *MIT Press. Cambridge, MA*.

Alessandro Moschitti. 2006. Efficient convolution kernels for dependency and constituent syntactic trees. In *Proceedings of The 17th European Conference on Machine Learning*, pages 318–329, Berlin, Germany.

Kai Wang and Zhaoyan Ming and Tat-Seng Chua. 2009. A Syntactic Tree Matching Approach to Finding Similar Questions in Community-based QA Services. In Proceedings of SIGIR, pages 187-194.

Roberto Basili, Marco Cammisa, and Alessandro Moschitti. 2005. Effective use of WordNet semantics via kernel-based learning. In *Proceedings of CoNLL-2005*, pages 1–8, Ann Arbor, Michigan. Association for Computational Linguistics.

Using a Recurrent Neural Network Model for Classification of Tweets Conveyed Influenza-related Information

Chen-Kai Wang[1], **Onkar Singh**[2,3] **Zhao-Li Tang**[1] and **Hong-Jie Dai**[4,5*]

[1]Graduate Institute of Biomedical Informatics, Taipei Medical University, Taipei, Taiwan, R.O.C.
[2]Bioinformatics Program, Taiwan International Graduate Program, Institute of Information Science, Academia Sinica, Taipei, Taiwan, R.O.C.
[3]Institute of Biomedical Informatics, National Yang-Ming University, Taipei, Taiwan, R.O.C.
[4]Department of Computer Science and Information Engineering, National Taitung University, Taitung, Taiwan, R.O.C.
[5]Interdisciplinary Program of Green and Information Technology, National Taitung University, Taitung, Taiwan, R.O.C.

Abstract

Traditional disease surveillance systems depend on outpatient reporting and virological test results released by hospitals. These data have valid and accurate information about emerging outbreaks but it's often not timely. In recent years the exponential growth of users getting connected to social media provides immense knowledge about epidemics by sharing related information. Social media can now flag more immediate concerns related to outbreaks in real time. In this paper we apply the long short-term memory recurrent neural network (RNN) architecture to classify tweets conveyed influenza-related information and compare its performance with baseline algorithms including support vector machine (SVM), decision tree, naive Bayes, simple logistics, and naive Bayes multinomial. The developed RNN model achieved an F-score of 0.845 on the MedWeb task test set, which outperforms the F-score of SVM without applying the synthetic minority oversampling technique by 0.08. The F-score of the RNN model is within 1% of the highest score achieved by SVM with oversampling technique.

1 Introduction

With the popularity of WWW, the use of data mining techniques to analyze the big data generated by users provides a feasible way for identification and exploration of health-related information. For example, Ginsberg et al. (2009) utilized search query logs of Google to develop models for influenza surveillance. With the recent increased use of social media platforms, users can communicate each other by updating their status led to wide sharing of personal information timely. The information spreads over these platforms is now a valuable information resource for building social sensors to develop real time event detection systems for detecting events like earthquakes (Sakaki, Okazaki, & Matsuo, 2010) and abuse of medications (Sarker, O'Connor, et al., 2016).

A review conducted by Charles-Smith et al. (2015) demonstrated evidence that the use of social media data can provide real-time surveillance of health issues, speed up outbreak management, identify target populations necessary to support and even improve public health and intervention outcomes. Facebook, microblogs, blogs, and discussion forums are examples of such media. Among them, Twitter, the leading micro-blogging platform, has become the primary data sources for digital disease surveillance and outbreak management. The

* Corresponding author

Proceedings of the International Workshop on Digital Disease Detection using Social Media 2017 (DDDSM-2017), pages 33–38,
Taipei, Taiwan, November 27, 2017.

platform has been used for creating first hand reports of adverse drug events (Bian, Topaloglu, & Yu, 2012). Shared tasks (Aramaki, Wakamiya, Morita, Kano, & Ohkuma, 2017; SARKER, NIKFARJAM, & GONZALEZ, 2016) and hackathon style competitions (Adam, Jonnagaddala, Chughtai, & Macintyre, 2017) for digital disease detection or biosurveillance are also emerging. The rationale behind social media-based surveillance systems is based on the assumption that target events occur in the real world will immediately reflect on social media. Therefore, systems that aggregate and determine the degree of related information from social media can monitor or even forecast the current or future outbreak events.

Iso, Wakamiya, and Aramaki (2016) have demonstrated words such as "fever" present clues for upcoming influenza outbreaks. They concluded that an approximately 16-day time lag exists between the frequency of the word "fever" mentioned in tweets and the number of influenza patients announced by the infectious disease surveillance center in Japan. Although their results are promising, the use of word-level information was noisy and impedes precise influenza surveillance. Take the following two tweets described in the work of Aramaki, Maskawa, and Morita (2011) as an example.

"*Headache? You might have flu.*"
"*The World Health Organization reports the avian influenza, or bird flu, epidemic has spread to nine Asian countries in the past few weeks.*"

Although the above two tweets include mentions of "flu", apparently they do not indicate any influenza patient has presented nearby. Therefore it is required to develop classifiers to categorize diseases/symptoms related to influenza in order to have an accurate influenza forecasting model. With this in mind, we consider to develop classifiers for diseases/symptoms related to influenza. We formulate the task as a classification problem and employ several baseline algorithms and recurrent neural networks (RNNs) to develop our models. The performance of the developed models are evaluated on a corpus annotated with eight disease/symptoms including influenza, cold, hay fever, diarrhea, headache, cough, fever and runny nose.

2 Method

2.1 Preprocessing

In the preprocessing step, we normalize all web links and usernames into "@URL" and "@REF" respectively. The part-of-speech tagger developed by Gimpel et al. (2011) is then used to tokenize tweets followed by removing the hashtag symbol "#" from its attached keywords or topics. Finally, we followed the numeric normalization procedure proposed by (Dai, Touray, Wang, Jonnagaddala, & Syed-Abdul, 2016) to normalize all numeral parts in each token into "1".

2.2 Network Architecture

The network architecture used in this study is a recurrent model consisting of an embedding layer, a bi-directional RNN layer followed by a dense layer to compute the posterior probabilities for each disease or symptom. Figure 1 illustrates the architecture.

2.3 Embedding Layer

The pre-trained word vectors for Twitter generated by GloVe (Pennington, Socher, & Manning, 2014) was used to initialize the embedding layer. The pre-trained 200-dimensional vectors were trained on two billion tweets which can be downloaded from the project website[2]. For word cannot be found in the pre-trained vectors, we initialized it with values closed to zero.

2.4 Recurrent Neural Network and Dense Layer

RNNs have proven to be a very powerful model in many natural language tasks (Mesnil, He, Deng, & Bengio, 2013; Tomá, Martin, Luká, Jan, & Sanjeev, 2010). This work used the long short term memory (LSTM), which is a special kind of RNN capable of learning long-term dependencies, to implement the RNN layer. As traditional RNNs, LSTM networks have the form of a chain of repeating cells of its neural network. LSTM uses gates to control the information flow inside its network. In Figure 1, assume that the first cell in the forward-LSTM is the tth token. The cell uses Equation 1 to output a value by considering the value h_{t-1} generated by the previous cell and the current input x_t.

$$f_t = \sigma(W_f \cdot [h_{t-1}, x_t] + b_f) \quad (1)$$

[2]https://nlp.stanford.edu/projects/glove/

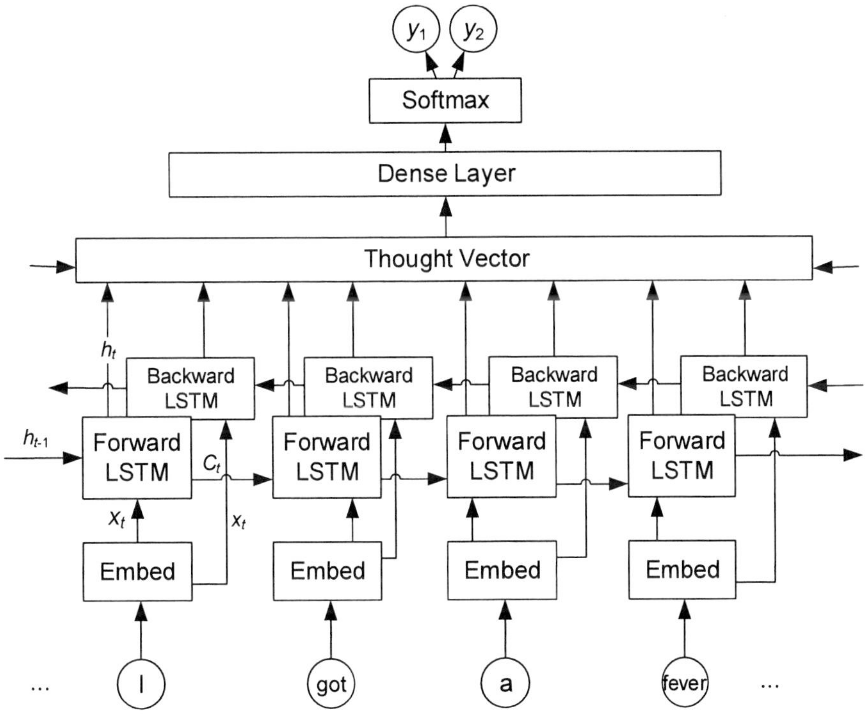

Figure 1: Network architecture developed in this work.

The cell then produces its two outputs C_t and h_t by using equation 4 and equation 6 respectively.

$$i_t = \sigma(W_i \cdot [h_{t-1}, x_t] + b_i) \quad (2)$$

$$\widetilde{C_t} = \tanh(W_C \cdot [h_{t-1}, x_t] + b_C) \quad (3)$$

$$C_t = f_t * C_{t-1} + i_t * \widetilde{C_t} \quad (4)$$

$$o_t = \sigma(W_o \cdot [h_{t-1}, x_t] + b_o) \quad (5)$$

$$h_t = o_t * \tanh(C_t) \quad (6)$$

In our network architecture, we duplicate the first recurrent layer to create a second recurrent layer so that there are now two layers side-by-side. The second layer is denoted as the Backward LSTM in Figure 1. For the backward layer, the input sequence is provided as a reversed copy of the input sequence.

Finally, we concatenate the last frame from the forward recursion, and the first frame from the backward recursion to build the thought vector (Gibson). The vector is then be the input of the dense layer with a dimension of 150 for soft max classification.

For the task studied in this work, we created one RNN model for each disease/symptom. Therefore, in total of eight RNN models were constructed for the eight types of diseases/symptoms.

2.5 Baseline Systems

Owing to the evaluation of the MedWeb task is ongoing, for the purpose of performance comparison, we implemented several baseline algorithms with Weka (Holmes, Donkin, & Witten, 1994) including C4.5 decision tree, simple logistic, support vector machine(SVM) trained with sequential minimal optimization, and Naïve Bayes Multinomial. The features used by the baseline were *n*-gram features with TF-IDF as the weighing function. Based on the tokens generated by the preprocessing step, we generate lowercased unigrams, bigrams and trigrams and filtered out stop words by using the list developed by McCallum (1996) along with a custom stop word list created by analyzing the training set. Finally, the Snowball stemmer (Porter, 2001) is used to perform stemming.

Symptom/Disease	Positive	Negative
Influenza	112	1808
Diarrhea	189	1731
Hay fever	201	1719
Cough	237	1683
Headache	254	1666
Cold	284	1636
Fever	355	1565
Runny nose	417	1503
Total	2049	13311

Table 1: Statistics of the training set.

3 Results

3.1 Dataset

The dataset released by NTCIR13-MedWeb task was used in this study (Kato, Kishida, Kando, Saka, & Sanderson, 2017). The dataset contains annotations indicating whether a Twitter user or someone around the user has symptoms or diseases like influenza, cold, hay fever, diarrhea, headache, cough, fever or runny nose at that point in time. Each tweet in the dataset was assigned with one of the following two labels. The label "p" (positive) is given if a tweet is determined as having symptom while the label "n" (negative) if it is not determined as a symptom/disease.

The training set consists of 1,920 tweets. Table 1 shows the statistics of the training set. As one can see that the dataset suffered the class imbalance problem.

3.2 Evaluation Metrics

We used the standard precision, recall and F-measure to evaluate the developed methods. We considered both the micro- and macro-averaged F-measure (Sokolova & Lapalme, 2009). A micro-F-score is generated by pooling all true positives, false positives and false negatives and calculate the F-score from that. A macro-average, on the other hand, is obtained by calculating the F-score for each class, and then averaging those F-scores to get a single number.

	P	R	F
SVM	0.869	0.880	0.875
C4.5	0.849	0.861	0.855
Naïve Bayes (NB)	0.262	0.966	0.413
Simple Logistic	0.822	0.924	0.870
NB Multinomial	0.666	0.874	0.756
SVM-SMOTE	0.867	0.882	0.875

Table 2: Baseline algorithm performance on the training set (micro-averaged).

	P	R	F
SVM	0.865	0.874	0.869
C4.5	0.841	0.851	0.845
Naïve Bayes (NB)	0.265	0.967	0.406
Simple Logistic	0.817	0.915	0.863
NB Multinomial	0.662	0.874	0.751
SVM-SMOTE	0.861	0.876	0.869

Table 3: Baseline algorithm performance on the training set (macro-averaged).

3.3 Results of the Baseline System on the Training Set

Table 2 and 3 show the two fold cross validation results on the English corpus of the MedWeb task. The baseline classifier with the best overall F-measure is SVM, which achieves the highest F-scores in the categories of "Cold" and "Influenza". The detail per-category performance of SVM is shown in Table 4.

Consider the imbalance observed in the training set, we try to increase the weight of examples when the classifiers makes errors on false positives. However the F-scores of all baseline classifiers didn't be improved. We also applied the synthetic minority oversampling technique (SMOTE) (Chawla, Bowyer, Hall, & Kegelmeyer, 2002) to create new instances for training SVM. The result is indicated by SVM-SMOTE in Table 2 and 3. We can observe that the precision and the recall is improved in micro-average and macro-average respectively. The overall F-score is also slightly improved.

	P	R	F
Influenza	0.746	0.759	0.752
Diarrhea	0.849	0.894	0.871
Hay fever	0.848	0.915	0.880
Cough	0.982	0.911	0.945
Headache	0.887	0.929	0.908
Cold	0.982	0.911	0.945
Fever	0.837	0.865	0.850
Runny nose	0.864	0.882	0.873

Table 4: Performance of the best performed baseline model on the training set.

Configuration	P	R	F
SVM	0.734	0.809	0.770
SVM-SMOTE	0.807	0.911	0.856
RNN	0.836	0.854	0.845

Table 5: Performance on the test set (micro-averaged).

3.4 Results on the Test Set

Table 5 and 6 show the performance of the two best performed baselines and the proposed RNN model on the test set of the MedWeb task. The developed RNN model can achieve an F-score of 0.845, which outperforms the F-score of the SVM model by 0.0754 and is closed to that of the best performed baseline SVM-SMOTE. Comparing SVM-SMOTE with the proposed RNN model, RNN has better precision while lower recall. We can also observe that the precision and recall of the developed RNN model has similar scores while SVM-based models have better recall.

3.5 Discussion

Because the organizers of the MedWeb task have not released the gold annotations for the test set, we cannot conduct in-depth error analysis on the test set. Herein, we list some important key terms for each symptoms/diseases based on the results of the training set in Table 7. The list is generated by using the tree structures of C4.5 to prioritize the important terms for each symptoms/diseases. In addition to the terms directly related to the corresponding symptoms/diseases, we can see some interesting terms like "dog" for runny nose and "Nepali" for diarrhea.

4 Conclusion

In this paper, we presented a neural network architecture based on a bi-directional RNNs that can classify tweets conveying influenza-related information. We study the performance of this architecture and compare it to the best performing baseline algorithm on the test set of the MedWeb

Configuration	P	R	F
SVM	0.733	0.835	0.770
SVM-SMOTE	0.796	0.918	0.849
RNN	0.818	0.844	0.828

Table 6: Performance on the test set (macro-averaged).

Type	Terms
Cold	cold, fever
Cough	coughing, cough, phlegm
Hayfever	because of, allergies, spring, pollen,
Headache	headache, head hurt
Influenza	flu, vaccinate
Runny-nose	nose, dog
Fever	temperature
Diarrhea	stomach, Nepali

Table 7: Key terms observed on the training set.

task. Using th e micro-F1 measure, the developed RNN model outperforms SVM by 0.087 and is within 1% of the highest score achieved by SVM with oversampling technique. In the future, we will continue to improve the performance of our model and conduct in depth error analysis regarding to the different symptoms/diseases.

References

Adam, D., Jonnagaddala, J., Chughtai, A. A., & Macintyre, C. R. (2017). *ZikaHack 2016: A digital disease detection competitio*. Paper presented at the Proceedings of the International Workshop on Digital Disease Detection using Social Media 2017, Taipei, Taiwan.

Aramaki, E., Maskawa, S., & Morita, M. (2011). *Twitter catches the flu: detecting influenza epidemics using Twitter*. Paper presented at the Proceedings of the conference on empirical methods in natural language processing.

Aramaki, E., Wakamiya, S., Morita, M., Kano, Y., & Ohkuma, T. (2017). *Overview of the NTCIR-13: MedWeb task*. Paper presented at the Proceeding of the NTCIR-13 Conference, Tokyo, Japan.

Bian, J., Topaloglu, U., & Yu, F. (2012). *Towards large-scale twitter mining for drug-related adverse events*. Paper presented at the Proceedings of the 2012 international workshop on Smart health and wellbeing.

Charles-Smith, L. E., Reynolds, T. L., Cameron, M. A., Conway, M., Lau, E. H. Y., Olsen, J. M., . . . Corley, C. D. (2015). Using Social Media for Actionable Disease Surveillance and Outbreak Management: A Systematic Literature Review. *PLoS ONE, 10*(10), e0139701. doi:10.1371/journal.pone.0139701

Chawla, N. V., Bowyer, K. W., Hall, L. O., & Kegelmeyer, W. P. (2002). SMOTE: synthetic minority over-sampling technique. *Journal of artificial intelligence research, 16*, 321-357.

Dai, H.-J., Touray, M., Wang, C.-K., Jonnagaddala, J., & Syed-Abdul, S. (2016). Feature Engineering for Recognizing Adverse Drug Reactions from Twitter Posts. *Information*.

Gibson, C. N., Adam. Thought Vectors, Deep Learning & the Future of AI - Deeplearning4j: Open-source, distributed deep learning for the JVM.

Gimpel, K., Schneider, N., O'Connor, B., Das, D., Mills, D., Eisenstein, J., . . . Smith, N. A. (2011). *Part-of-speech tagging for Twitter: annotation, features, and experiments*. Paper presented at the Proceedings of the 49th Annual Meeting of the Association for Computational Linguistics: Human Language Technologies: short papers - Volume 2, Portland, Oregon.

Ginsberg, J., Mohebbi, M. H., Patel, R. S., Brammer, L., Smolinski, M. S., & Brilliant, L. (2009). Detecting influenza epidemics using search engine query data. *Nature, 457*(7232), 1012-1014.

Holmes, G., Donkin, A., & Witten, I. H. (1994). *Weka: A machine learning workbench.* Paper presented at the Intelligent Information Systems, 1994. Proceedings of the 1994 Second Australian and New Zealand Conference on.

Iso, H., Wakamiya, S., & Aramaki, E. (2016, December 11-17). *Forecasting Word Model: Twitter-based Influenza Surveillance and Prediction.* Paper presented at the Proceedings of the 26th International Conference on Computational Linguistics, Osaka, Japan.

Kato, M. P., Kishida, K., Kando, N., Saka, T., & Sanderson, M. (2017). *Report on NTCIR-12: The Twelfth Round of NII Testbeds and Community for Information Access Research.* Paper presented at the ACM SIGIR Forum.

McCallum, A. K. (1996). Bow: A toolkit for statistical language modeling, text retrieval, classification and clustering. *http://www.cs.cmu.edu/~mccallum/bow.*

Mesnil, G., He, X., Deng, L., & Bengio, Y. (2013). *Investigation of recurrent-neural-network architectures and learning methods for spoken language understanding.* Paper presented at the INTERSPEECH.

Pennington, J., Socher, R., & Manning, C. D. (2014). Glove: Global vectors for word representation. *Proceedings of the Empiricial Methods in Natural Language Processing (EMNLP 2014), 12*, 1532-1543.

Porter, M. F. (2001). Snowball: A language for stemming algorithms. Retrieved from http://snowball.tartarus.org/texts/introduction.html

Sakaki, T., Okazaki, M., & Matsuo, Y. (2010). *Earthquake shakes Twitter users: real-time event detection by social sensors.* Paper presented at the Proceedings of the 19th international conference on World wide web.

SARKER, A., NIKFARJAM, A., & GONZALEZ, G. (2016). *SOCIAL MEDIA MINING SHARED TASK WORKSHOP.* Paper presented at the Pacific Symposium on Biocomputing 2016.

Sarker, A., O'Connor, K., Ginn, R., Scotch, M., Smith, K., Malone, D., & Gonzalez, G. (2016). Social Media Mining for Toxicovigilance: Automatic Monitoring of Prescription Medication Abuse from Twitter. *Drug Safety, 39*(3), 231-240. doi:10.1007/s40264-015-0379-4

Sokolova, M., & Lapalme, G. (2009). A systematic analysis of performance measures for classification tasks. *Information Processing & Management, 45*(4), 427-437.

Tomá, M., Martin, K., Luká, B., Jan, È., & Sanjeev, K. (2010). *Recurrent neural network based language model.* Paper presented at the Proceedings of the 11th Annual Conference of the International Speech Communication Association, Makuhari, Chiba, Japan.

ZikaHack 2016: A digital disease detection competition

Dillon C Adam[1], Jitendra Jonnagaddala[2], Daniel Han-Chen[3], Sean Batongbacal[4], Luan Almeida[5], Jing Z Zhu[6], Jenny J Yang[7], Jumail M Mundekkat[4], Steven Badman[8], Abrar A Chughtai[1], C Raina MacIntyre[1]

[1]Integrated Systems for Epidemic Response, UNSW Sydney, Australia
[2]School of Public Health, UNSW Sydney, Australia
[3]School of Mathematics & Statistics, UNSW Sydney, Australia
[4]School of Computer Science & Engineering, UNSW Sydney, Australia
[5]Computer Science Department, Federal University of Alagoas, Brazil
[6]Concord Repatriation General Hospital, Sydney, Australia
[7]Faculty of Medicine, UNSW Sydney, Australia
[8]Kirby Institute, UNSW Sydney, Australia

Abstract

Effective response to infectious diseases outbreaks relies on the rapid and early detection of those outbreaks. Invalidated, yet timely and openly available digital information can be used for the early detection of outbreaks. Public health surveillance authorities can exploit these early warnings to plan and co-ordinate rapid surveillance and emergency response programs. In 2016, a digital disease detection competition named ZikaHack was launched. The objective of the competition was for multidisciplinary teams to design, develop and demonstrate innovative digital disease detection solutions to retrospectively detect the 2015-16 Brazilian Zika virus outbreak earlier than traditional surveillance methods. In this paper, an overview of the ZikaHack competition is provided. The challenges and lessons learned in organizing this competition are also discussed for use by other researchers interested in organizing similar competitions.

1 Introduction

Rapid detection of disease outbreaks through disease surveillance is critical for early and effective prevention and control of potential epidemics. Traditional communicable disease surveillance typically includes elements of case detection, validation, and dissemination, to accurately detect outbreaks and inform subsequent control measures where necessary. These methods however, while highly specific, rely on clinical diagnoses and/or laboratory confirmation, and involve a chain of processing from health providers to government health authorities. This can be a time-consuming process, which while suitable for accurate surveillance of long term trends, is not timely enough for rapid outbreak detection. More timely methods of detecting outbreaks could reduce the delay of disease control measures, particularly important during the early hours and days of an outbreak.

The extraordinary increase in public domain data driven by the accessibility of the internet, smart phones and social media, mean that a wealth of information about our individual and collective lives is more readily available than ever before. Utilizing these data for disease surveillance is referred to as digital disease detection. It has shown increasing promise in the early detection and identification of outbreaks, despite concerns regarding the validity and accuracy of disease predictions (Bernardo et al., 2013; Chunara et al., 2012). Despite these limitations, unofficial public data sources, such as online search engines and social media can provide timely information for the early detection of disease outbreaks and can be used to support the early initiation of traditional surveillance activities (Bernardo et al., 2013; Ginsberg et

Proceedings of the International Workshop on Digital Disease Detection using Social Media 2017 (DDDSM-2017), pages 39–46,
Taipei, Taiwan, November 27, 2017. ©2017 AFNLP

al., 2009; Salathe et al., 2013). The World Health Organization (WHO) reports that more than 60% of their initial outbreak reports come from unofficial sources (Christaki, 2015; World Health Organization, 2016).

1.1 Zika & the 2015 Brazilian outbreak

Zika virus (ZIKV) was first identified in monkeys in 1947, and then in humans in 1952 in Uganda (Kirya, 1977). Only occasionally reported in equatorial regions of Africa and Asia (Ioos et al., 2014), the virus was not considered a pathogen of significant public health concern until the 2015 epidemic in Brazil, concurrent with reports of associations with birth defects such as microcephaly. The first signs of a potential ZIKV outbreak occurred in May 2015, as the Pan American Health Organization (PAHO) released an alert for possible ZIKV infection in Brazil following a cluster of non-specific rash in February 2015. The first cluster of microcephaly cases was reported in August 2015 but the association with ZIKV infection wasn't noted until November (Schuler-Faccini et al., 2016). By February 2016, the World Health Organization (WHO) declared the ZIKV epidemic to be a Public Health Emergency of International Concern (World Health Organization (WHO), 2016). It is estimated that anywhere between 10–80% of the Brazilian population (207 million) may have been exposed to ZIKV during the outbreak (Jaenisch et al., 2016; Johansson et al., 2016; Nishiura et al., 2016). If symptoms do appear, they are mostly mild and non-specific such as such as fever, rash, and joint pain typical of many other arboviral diseases such as dengue and chikungunya (Duffy et al., 2009; Grard et al., 2014; Olson et al., 1981). As such, many women were not aware they had become infected until their baby was born with birth defects nine months later. The risk of microcephaly due to ZIKV is estimated to be low, ranging from 0-5%, but may be as high as 30% (Jaenisch et al., 2016; Johansson et al., 2016; Nishiura et al., 2016; Oliveira Melo et al., 2016; Ventura et al., 2016).

2 ZikaHack 2016

Hackathons are typically short-term competitions which bring together multidisciplinary teams to develop innovative solutions to a defined problem. Hackathon style competitions have proven effective in enhancing student-centred learning and fostering inter professional development (Kienzler & Fontanesi, 2017; Youm & Wiechmann, 2015). Inspired by this, a digital disease detection competition called 'ZikaHack 2016' was organised and sponsored by The National Health and Medical Research Council's (NHMRC) Centre for Research Excellence in Integrated Systems for Epidemic Response (ISER)[1]. Based at University of New South Wales (UNSW) Sydney, ISER conducts applied systems research to enhance collaboration and build capacity in health systems for epidemic response and control. Open to university students world-wide, the competition challenged multidisciplinary student teams to design and develop digital disease detection solutions to detect early signals for the ZIKV outbreak in Brazil earlier than traditionally surveillance methods did, using only publicly available data sources. One of the main task for the teams was to identify the Brazilian ZIKV outbreak and formulate the scope for potential early signals.

3 Competition structure

3.1 Overview

The competition was split into two phases: a shortlisting phase, and a development phase. Phase one of the competition was launched in August 2016. Eligible teams of three to six students were tasked to submit an application including a proposal of no more than 3,000 words describing their solution to detect an early ZIKV surveillance signal. A key requirement for entry was the cross-disciplinary background and mixed study level of the student teams: team composition had to include both undergraduate and postgraduate students with at least one student from science, technology, engineering or math (STEM), and another from a health-related program. Students had to be enrolled at a recognised university within their country at the time of application. Only applications in English were accepted. For exact eligibility criteria used, please refer to Appendix A.

Details of the competition such as conditions of entry and proposal requirements were posted on the

[1] https://sphcm.med.unsw.edu.au/centres-units/centre-research-excellence-epidemic-response

ISER website. The competition was widely publicized on the university website and emails were sent to colleagues working at other universities in Australia and overseas for promotion. A local company, thinkable.org, was also contracted to promote and field applicants for the competition.

3.1 Phase One

Phase one of the competition was launched in August 2016. Students were given approximately five months to form teams and submit a proposal before the closing date of 30 November 2016. Applications were reviewed for eligibility and ranked in a blinded process by a panel of four judges independently. Criteria for the ranking was general: a demonstrated understanding of the ZIKV problem in Brazil, the contest brief and originality of the proposed solution. A median-rank score for each submission was calculated blindly and submissions re-ranked. Judges deliberated over the top performing submissions and selected two finalists to move forward into phase two. Teams were notified on 19 December 2016. A summary of phase one proposals is presented in Table 1.

3.2 Phase Two

Teams shortlisted for phase two were tasked to begin development and implementation of their proposed digital disease detection solutions. The primary criteria for evaluation was the ability of the solution to identify the ZIKV outbreak early compared to the official ZKV epidemic alert by the WHO in February 2016. Complete solution documentation and source code were also required to be compiled for evaluation. A joint teleconference with the finalists and the competition organizers was held to provide teams with an opportunity to ask questions and discuss any challenges faced. Final submissions were due 30 April 2017. The finalists presented an overview of their solutions and early signals of ZIKV outbreak in Brazil before the same four person judging panel. Presentations were scored according to a final criterion including the ability of the tool to produce an early signal of the ZIKV outbreak earlier than traditional surveillance, originality, feasibility and adaptability of the design. The winning team was notified in early May 2017[2].

4 Competition results

4.1 Participants

A total of eight proposals were received in phase one. One team was disqualified as they did not meet the entry criteria. Of the seven qualifying teams, the average team size was five persons with 34 total individual student applicants. The large majority student applicants were enrolled at an Australian university (n=32; 94%) and male (n=26; 77.5%). Four out of seven teams collaborated between at least two universities with the remaining three team's composition exclusively of students from the same university. The most common level of study was postgraduate (n=22; 65%) and of those, most were enrolled in a Master level program (n=16; 73%) followed by a doctoral level program (n=6; 27%). Thirty-five percent of applicants were (n=12) enrolled in an undergraduate bachelor program. Across all program levels, public health and computer science were the most common fields of study (n=6; 18% each) followed by data science, information technologies and engineering (n=5; 15% each).

4.2 Proposed solutions

Most but not all teams correctly understood the challenge of identifying early signals of Brazilian ZIKV outbreak. Teams routinely proposed using machine learning and natural language processing algorithms to develop models for ZIKV prediction from social media sources. However, the queries used and data sources specified differed between teams as did the methods. At least one social media platform was chosen by most teams as a potential data source for digital disease detection however in some cases multiple sources were specified. The most common source was Twitter (n=5/7; 71%), followed by Facebook (n=3/7; 42%). The 'REST' and 'Streaming Twitter' API was commonly proposed (even though it is not possible to obtain the data required for this competition retrospectively) as a means for data extraction. Google trends was another source of data proposed (n=3/7; 47%). Some common query-terms proposed across social

[2] https://newsroom.unsw.edu.au/news/health/students-find-early-signals-zika-virus-outbreak

Team	Data Sources	Algorithms	Language
1	Facebook, Google search, National weather data, Census data	Unnamed machine learning algorithms, Delay differential, Proportional hazards models	Not specified
2	Twitter, PubMed, Google scholar, News sources, Worldclim.org	Unnamed mosquito model, SIR transmission model	Python
3	Facebook, Twitter, Google trends, Google maps, National weather statistics, Mass social events calendar, Wikipedia, HealthMap, CDC	Deep neural networks, Unnamed machine learning algorithms.	Python, R, Matlab
4	United Nations world tourism organisation, Government reports	Unnamed clustering algorithm, Random forests, Decision trees.	Python, R
5	Twitter, Global climate data, Google trends	Bayesian Markov network model, Auto regression exogenous model, SVM regression model, Naive Bayes	Not specified
6	Twitter	Deep neural networks	Python
7	Reddit, Twitter, Wikipedia, Instagram	Deep neural networks, Unnamed aberration detection models	Python

Table 1: Summary of phase one proposals

media platforms and search engines included: fever, rash, headache and conjunctivitis. Python was mentioned in all proposed solutions that specified at least one programming language, followed by R and Matlab.

Proposed solutions for ZIKV early detection varied and are summarised in Table 1. Many teams included climate variables into their models as a predictor of mosquito biting risk. For example, Team 1 proposed using an algorithm to predict ideal conditions for a ZIKV outbreak based on historic climate data (mosquito risk) and calculating outliers of a regression analysis using filtered search results. Another incorporated the epidemiological concept of R_0 (expected number of secondary infection produced by primary infection) by calculating the predicted number of ZIKV infections by location using a trained machine learning model from twitter data, and then statistically compared this value to other models with similar symptoms such as dengue and chikungunya. Some solutions however demonstrated a collection of ideas that lacked detail or were inappropriate for desired challenge outcome. Two of the proposed solutions were selected for phase two development.

4.3 Winning Solution: Gadyan

Gadyan (in Australian aboriginal language means "Sydney shellfish") was able to generate early signals, approximately three months before the WHO official alert in early 2016. Gadyan employed a multi-stage pipeline based approach with various components and sub-components incorporated into the solution. Gadyan specifically focused on microcephaly syndromic surveillance and used retrospectively collected relevant data from Google trends, Twitter and Wikipedia for the period Jan 2013 to December 2016. The data extracted from these sources varied in type and formats. Unstructured tweets were extracted from twitter users in Brazil and structured data from the Google trends and Wikipedia. As part of this solution, automatic translation was also performed on Portuguese and Spanish data. The data extracted from these various heterogeneous data sources were appropriately represented in standardized time series (weekly intervals and monthly) formats. The standardized data was further used to generate outbreak alerts. Initially, the alerts were generated using a single data source and conventional aberration detection algorithms. However, the better early warning alerts were possible by combining all the data sources and using change point detection algorithms instead of standard aberration detection algorithms. The official microcephaly surveillance data from WHO/PAHO was used to perform correlation analysis and assessment of the outbreak alerts during the development of the solution. The developed Gadyan solution is subjected to various limitations but can be extended to detect other disease outbreaks.

4.4 Runner Up

The second finalist and runner-up developed an Outbreak Confidence Distribution (OCD) model to compute the likelihood of a ZIKV outbreak by location (Brazilian states). The solution used a combination of retrospective google search term queries downloaded in both Spanish and Portuguese to train a stacked Machine Learning model with Random Forests and Neural Nets. The model was trained on data sourced from three Brazilian states and then tested on the remaining states. The solution produced signals of possible ZIKV outbreak as early as September 2014 in the state of Espírito Santo. The early signal of ZIKV varied for each state, but the model commonly identified November 2014 as the potential origin of the outbreak in Brazil. The solution however suffered from some noisy signals.

5 Discussion

The results demonstrate that student-centred multi-disciplinary teams can provide unique and innovative solutions to challenging digital disease detection problems. There are many advantages in carrying out competitions such as this in an academic setting. Hackathons are frequently reported as hubs for student research innovations (Artiles & Wallace, 2013; Briscoe, 2014) and the results of ZikaHack concur that university organised competitions with prize monies can incentivise talented students to apply for university competitions. Overall, the number of unique solutions proposed satisfied the goals of competition organisers.

Twitter as the choice source of public domain data was unsurprising. Many past efforts to create digital disease detection (DDD) tools have used Twitter as a primary data source to track epidemics (Aramaki et al., 2011; Jonnagaddala et al., 2016; Lampos et al., 2010). Despite its popularity, the effectiveness of twitter for DDD is questionable. For users, only 1% of the data can be publicly accessed (0.2% of which is geocoded), query terms used to retrieve data can lead to bias, and most tweets originate from the United States (Al-garadi et al., 2016; Romano et al., 2016). In addition, Twitter is also a very difficult source to perform microcephaly syndromic surveillance because identification of pregnant women on social media is a challenging task (Huang et al., 2017). Google search trends can also suffer from similar biases. However, many proposals attempted to overcome issues of bias by integrating additional data such as climate into their models or weighting certain parameters and data points over others. For example, tweets that referenced rash and conjunctivitis would be weighted more than headache or haemorrhage due to their greater association with ZIKV infection compared with similar syndromes caused by chikungunya virus and dengue. This was recognised correctly as the primary challenge in identifying an early ZIKV signal by most teams.

The popularity of Python as the programming language of choice by teams was also unsurprising. It is well agreed that Python's relatively easy syntax, speed, and vast array of available libraries are particularly suited for DDD. Python as a language for data science and machine learning has recently surpassed R and all signs point to this trend continuing (Granville, 2017). While no restrictions on programming language was specified in the ZikaHack competition documents, if a single language is preferred to potentially ease administration and judging, future organisers should feel comfortable selecting Python.

We observed various issues and challenges in organising the ZikaHack competition. The eligibility requirements may have proved a barrier to some applicants, specifically, the requirement that students need to form a multi-disciplinary team of three to six members. Despite a comfortable application period, some interested students struggled to form teams and contacted the organisers to enquire about potential exemptions. While no exceptions were offered, a Facebook group and event page was organised shortly after launch to help students or single-discipline groups find potential team mates. The idea of using social media platform proved effective and we observed good engagement and communication between interested students. Those considering organising similar cross-disciplinary competitions would be advised to consider the use of social media to stimulate collaborations prior to launch.

Following the close of phase one and as the competition progressed into phase two, it became clear during that workloads were shared unevenly across teams, and often substantial contributions were from single students. In one instance, 70% of the work was formally declared as the work of a single team member, with as little as 5% coming from another in the same team. In another case, planning, formulation, and implementation of the digital disease detection models was the responsibility of one student, and all other team members declared equal responsibility for reviewing the model implementation and background. This may be evidence of a heavy technical burden required from computer science or engineering students to complete the challenge, and may have reduced the number of proposals submitted, however this cannot be proven. With this in mind, future competitions like ZikaHack with specific cross-disciplinary entry requirements may consider specifying a maximum and minimum declared workload per student to improve workload balance. Alternatively, loosening the multidisciplinary team requirements may improve balance but might also have adverse effects, such as a lack of understanding of the core challenges, in this case specifically related to ZIKV and health. The entry requirements in ZikaHack however were not without purpose: as mentioned, one of the primary goals of ISER (competition organiser) is to enhance collaboration and build capacity in health systems research for epidemic response and control. As such, it was important that there was cross-disciplinary engagement across student faculties, particularly between health and STEM, and to advocate cross-faculty research in the various areas of disease surveillance.

Female student participation was low in ZikaHack. Twenty-four percent (8/34) of all individual student applicants was female. Approximately 18% of current Australian Information Technology, Engineering and related technology students are female (Australian Government Department of Education and Training, 2017). We could therefore expect a similar distribution of gender across entries. While 24% of all applicants were female, 91% were from health-related fields meaning only 9% of female applicants were from computer science and engineering related areas. Studies have shown female participation in hackathons are significantly underrepresented when compared to enrolments (Richard et al., 2015), the reasons for which are not well examined, but may be symptomatic of the broader cultural challenges faced by females in predominately male fields such as reduced confidence, prejudice and stereotyping (Irani, 2004). Others suggest the underlying cause may be similar to societies' wider issues of underrepresentation of female computer science and engineering graduates employed in industry and academia. (Briscoe, 2014) Efforts to increasing the gender diversity in hackathon style competitions may therefore benefit from diversity quotas which may help resolve this imbalance. Alternatively, explicitly encouraging female entrants may reduce feelings of being unwelcome and the perceptions of a 'boys-club' (Warner & Guo, 2017). The reasons for reduced female participation in ZikaHack however is purely speculative, as participants were not interviewed.

6 Conclusion

ZikaHack 2016 was a unique, rewarding and successful adaption of the hackathon format and could be replicated yearly either as a continuation, by building on the work of previous years, or a source for new ideas by varying the specific challenge. As a competition with multi-disciplinary requirements, ZikaHack exposed students to concepts outside their field of study, which in turn may inspire participants into alternative research areas; for example, the proposals submitted here could serve as a platform for a future research proposals. In the case of ZikaHack, while never the original goal, research opportunities were offered to some finalists who exceeded expectations. Academics considering organising similar events might also consider how such competitions, perhaps organised yearly with associated monies, may initiate and sustain their areas of research into the future.

Acknowledgments

Funding for this competition was provided by the National health and medical research council's

Centre for Research Excellence, Integrated Systems for Epidemic Response (ISER), grant number APP1107393.

References

Al-garadi, Mohammed Ali, Khan, Muhammad Sadiq, Varathan, Kasturi Dewi, Mujtaba, Ghulam, & Al-Kabsi, Abdelkodose M. (2016). Using online social networks to track a pandemic: A systematic review. *Journal of Biomedical Informatics, 62*, 1-11.

Aramaki, Eiji, Maskawa, Sachiko, & Morita, Mizuki. (2011). *Twitter catches the flu: detecting influenza epidemics using Twitter.* Paper presented at the Proceedings of the conference on empirical methods in natural language processing.

Artiles, Jessica A, & Wallace, David R. (2013). Borrowing from hackathons: overnight designathons as a template for creative idea hubs in the space of hands-on learning, digital learning, and systems re-thinking. *WEEF, Cartagena.*

Australian Government Department of Education and Training (2017). uCube: Enrolment Count by Field Of Education by Gender. Retrieved from http://highereducationstatistics.education.gov.au/

Bernardo, T. M., Rajic, A., Young, I., Robiadek, K., Pham, M. T., & Funk, J. A. (2013). Scoping review on search queries and social media for disease surveillance: a chronology of innovation. *Journal of Medical Internet Research, 15*(7), e147.

Briscoe, Gerard. (2014). Digital innovation: The hackathon phenomenon.

Christaki, E. (2015). New technologies in predicting, preventing and controlling emerging infectious diseases. *Virulence, 6*(6), 558-565.

Chunara, R., Andrews, J. R., & Brownstein, J. S. (2012). Social and news media enable estimation of epidemiological patterns early in the 2010 Haitian cholera outbreak. *American Journal of Tropical Medicine & Hygiene, 86*(1), 39-45.

Duffy, Mark R., Chen, Tai-Ho, Hancock, W. Thane, Powers, Ann M., Kool, Jacob L., Lanciotti, Robert S., . . . Hayes, Edward B. (2009). Zika Virus Outbreak on Yap Island, Federated States of Micronesia. *New England Journal of Medicine, 360*(24), 2536-2543.

Ginsberg, J., Mohebbi, MH., Patel, RS., Brammer, L., Smolinski, MS., & Brilliant, L. (2009). Detecting influenza epidemics using search engine query data. *Nature, 457*, 1012-1015.

Granville, V. (2017, August 30 2017). Python Overtakes R for Data Science and Machine Learning. Retrieved from http://www.datasciencecentral.com/profiles/blogs/python-overtakes-r-for-data-science-and-machine-learning

Grard, G., Caron, M., Mombo, I. M., Nkoghe, D., Mboui Ondo, S., Jiolle, D., . . . Leroy, E. M. (2014). Zika virus in Gabon (Central Africa)--2007: a new threat from Aedes albopictus? *PLoS Negl Trop Dis, 8*(2), e2681.

Huang, Yi-Jie , Su, Chu Hsien , Chang, Yi-Chun , Ting, Tseng-Hsin , Fu, Tzu-Yuan , Wang, Rou-Min , . . . Hsu, Wen-Lian. (2017). *Incorporating Dependency Trees Improve Identification of Pregnant Women on Social Media Platforms.* Paper presented at the Proceedings of the International Workshop on Digital Disease Detection using Social Media 2017, Taipei, Taiwan.

Ioos, S., Mallet, H. P., Leparc Goffart, I., Gauthier, V., Cardoso, T., & Herida, M. (2014). Current Zika virus epidemiology and recent epidemics. *Medecine et Maladies Infectieuses, 44*(7), 302-307.

Irani, Lilly. (2004). *Understanding gender and confidence in CS course culture.* Paper presented at the ACM SIGCSE Bulletin.

Jaenisch, Thomas, Rosenberger, Kerstin Daniela, Brito, Carlos, Brady, Oliver, Brasil, Patrícia, & Marques, Ernesto. (2016). Estimating the risk for microcephaly after Zika virus infection in Brazil. *Bulletin of the World Health Organization.*

Johansson, M. A., Mier-y-Teran-Romero, L., Reefhuis, J., Gilboa, S. M., & Hills, S. L. (2016). Zika and the Risk of Microcephaly. *New England Journal of Medicine, 375*(1), 1-4.

Jonnagaddala, Jitendra, Jue, Toni Rose , & Dai, Hong-Jie. (2016). *Binary classification of Twitter posts for adverse drug reactions.* Paper presented at the Proceedings of the Social Media Mining Shared Task Workshop at the Pacific Symposium on Biocomputing, Big Island, HI, USA.

Kienzler, Hanna, & Fontanesi, Carolyn. (2017). Learning through inquiry: a Global Health Hackathon. *Teaching in Higher Education, 22*(2), 129-142.

Kirya, B. G. (1977). A yellow fever epizootic in Zika forest, Uganda, during 1972: Part 1: Virus isolation and sentinel monkeys. *Trans R Soc Trop Med Hyg, 71*(3), 254-260.

Lampos, Vasileios, De Bie, Tijl, & Cristianini, Nello. (2010). Flu detector-tracking epidemics on Twitter. *Machine Learning and Knowledge Discovery in Databases*, 599-602.

Nishiura, H., Mizumoto, K., Rock, K. S., Yasuda, Y., Kinoshita, R., & Miyamatsu, Y. (2016). A theoretical estimate of the risk of microcephaly during pregnancy with Zika virus infection. *Epidemics, 15*, 66-70.

Oliveira Melo, A. S., Malinger, G., Ximenes, R., Szejnfeld, P. O., Alves Sampaio, S., & Bispo De Filippis, A. M. (2016). Zika virus intrauterine infection causes fetal brain abnormality and microcephaly: Tip of the iceberg? *Ultrasound in Obstetrics and Gynecology, 47*(1), 6-7.

Olson, J. G., Ksiazek, T. G., Suhandiman, & Triwibowo. (1981). Zika virus, a cause of fever in Central Java, Indonesia. *Trans R Soc Trop Med Hyg, 75*(3), 389-393.

Richard, Gabriela T, Kafai, Yasmin B, Adleberg, Barrie, & Telhan, Orkan. (2015). *StitchFest: Diversifying a College Hackathon to broaden participation and perceptions in computing.* Paper presented at the Proceedings of the 46th ACM Technical Symposium on Computer Science Education.

Romano, Sara, Di Martino, Sergio, Kanhabua, Nattiya, Mazzeo, Antonino, & Nejdl, Wolfgang. (2016). *Challenges in detecting epidemic outbreaks from social networks.* Paper presented at the Advanced Information Networking and Applications Workshops (WAINA), 2016 30th International Conference on.

Salathe, M., Freifeld, C. C., Mekaru, S. R., Tomasulo, A. F., & Brownstein, J. S. (2013). Influenza A (H7N9) and the importance of digital epidemiology. *New England Journal of Medicine, 369*(5), 401-404.

Schuler-Faccini, L., Ribeiro, E. M., Feitosa, I. M., Horovitz, D. D., Cavalcanti, D. P., Pessoa, A., . . . Brazilian Medical Genetics Society-Zika Embryopathy Task, Force. (2016). Possible Association Between Zika Virus Infection and Microcephaly - Brazil, 2015. *MMWR Morb Mortal Wkly Rep, 65*(3), 59-62.

Ventura, C. V., Maia, M., Bravo-Filho, V., Góis, A. L., & Belfort, R., Jr. (2016). Zika virus in Brazil and macular atrophy in a child with microcephaly. *The Lancet, 387*(10015), 228.

Warner, Jeremy, & Guo, Philip J. (2017). *Hack. edu: Examining How College Hackathons Are Perceived By Student Attendees and Non-Attendees.* Paper presented at the Proceedings of the 2017 ACM Conference on International Computing Education Research.

World Health Organization. (2016). Epidemic intelligence - systematic event detection. . Retrieved from http://www.who.int/csr/alertresponse/epidemicintelligence/en/

World Health Organization (WHO). (2016). WHO statement on the first meeting of the International Health Regulations (2005) (IHR 2005) Emergency Committee on Zika virus and observed increase in neurological disorders and neonatal malformations. Retrieved from http://www.who.int/mediacentre/news/statements/2016/1st-emergency-committee-zika/en/

Youm, J., & Wiechmann, W. (2015). The Med AppJam: a model for an interprofessional student-centered mHealth app competition. *J Med Syst, 39*(3), 34.

Appendix A. Eligibility Criteria

The following eligibility Criteria was used for the ZikaHack 2016 competition.

- Student team has 3 to 6 enrolled students (who must all be enrolled at the time of the Phase 1 Submission Date of 30 November 2016)
- There is a single nominated team leader
- Team includes undergraduate and postgraduate students
- Team includes students from the following two discipline areas: STEM (science, technology, engineering, mathematics) and health related (medicine, nursing, public health, allied health) disciplines
- Must be studying at a registered university and recognised within its country as a university.
- Letter of support including verification of the student's status of enrolment using the template provided for each team member is attached to the application.
- Application in English
- No team member had a direct connection with any investigator or affiliate of ISER (such as a student-supervisor relationship)
- The work has been done entirely by the student team, with no other assistance.
- All students agreed to be named as part of the team

A Method to Generate a Machine-Labeled Data for Biomedical Named Entity Recognition with Various Sub-Domains

Juae Kim[1], Sunjae Kwon[1], Youngjoong Ko[2], and Jungyun Seo[1]
Computer Science, Sogang University, Sinsu-dong 1, Mapo-gu, Seoul, Korea[1]
Computer Engineering, Dong-A University, 840 Hadan 2-dong, Saha-gu, Busan, Korea[2]
{juaekim, soon91jae , seojy}@sogang.ac.kr[1],
yungjoong.ko@gmail.com[2]

Abstract

Biomedical Named Entity (NE) recognition is a core technique for various works in the biomedical domain. In previous studies, using machine learning algorithm shows better performance than dictionary-based and rule based approaches because there are too many terminological variations of biomedical NEs and new biomedical NEs are constantly generated. To achieve the high performance with a machine-learning algorithm, good-quality corpora are required. However, it is difficult to obtain the good-quality corpora because annotating a biomedical corpus for machine-learning is extremely time-consuming and costly. In addition, most previous corpora are insufficient for high-level tasks because they cannot cover various domains. Therefore, we propose a method for generating a large amount of machine-labeled data that covers various domains. To generate a large amount of machine-labeled data, firstly we generate an initial machine-labeled data by using a chunker and MetaMap. The chunker is developed to extract only biomedical NEs with manually annotated data. MetaMap is used to annotate the category of biomedical NE. Then we apply the self-training approach to bootstrap the performance of initial machine-labeled data. In our experiments, the biomedical NE recognition system that is trained with our proposed machine-labeled data achieves much high performance. As a result, our system outperforms biomedical NE recognition system that using MetaMap only with 26.03%p improvements on F1-score.

1 Introduction

As biomedical research has been actively studied, the attention of bioinformatics with natural language processing is rapidly increasing. According to generate an amount of data in the biomedical domain, to extract and retrieval the high-quality information is increasingly important (Zeng et al., 2015). Then, extracting the Biomedical Named Entity (biomedical NE) is also important to comprehend the biomedical text. There are two steps to extract biomedical NEs. The first step is an identification of biomedical entities from text. Second, biomedical entities that identified are classified into some several categories such as protein, drug, cell-line, and disease. These categories provide useful information to high-level applications. To extract the biomedical NEs are considered challenging task because there are too many terminological variations of biomedical NEs and new biomedical NEs are constantly generated with the course of time. That is why studies using machine learning show higher performance that dictionary or rule based approaches. There are many efforts that extract a high-quality biomedical NEs. (Robert et al., 2015) suggests a chemical named entity recognizer implemented by combining two independent machine learning models. (Li et al., 2015), (Li et al., 2016) apply the latest technology which is deep learning. The named entity recognizer of (Li et al., 2015), (Li et al., 2016) are based on Recurrent Neural Network and LSTM. However, annotating a biomedical corpus for machine-learning is extremely time-consuming and costly because of the requirement of medical experts. In addition, most previous corpora are insufficient for high-level application likes question answering (QA) system that requires various biomedical information. Because biomedical NE cat-

Proceedings of the International Workshop on Digital Disease Detection using Social Media 2017 (DDDSM-2017), pages 47–51,
Taipei, Taiwan, November 27, 2017.

Category (abbreviation)	Category (UMLS semantic groups)
ACTI	Activities & Behaviors
ANAT	Anatomy
CHEM	Chemicals & Drugs
CONC	Concepts & Ideas
DEVI	Devices
DISO	Disorders
GENE	Genes & Molecular Sequences
GEOG	Geographic Areas
LIVB	Living Beings
OBJC	Objects
OCCU	Occupations
ORGA	Organizations
PHEN	Phenomena
PHYS	Physiology
PROC	Procedures

Table 1: UNLS semantic groups

egories were limited to specific sub-domains of biomedicine in each corpus. For example, the biomedical NE recognition system that trained with GENIA corpus (Kim et al., 2003), only cover the gene and protein subdomain.

Therefore, we propose a method for creating the automatically labeled corpus that covers various domains. The biomedical NE recognition system that is trained with our proposed machine-labeled corpus can extract biomedical NEs in various domains.

We utilize the open source biomedical NE recognition tool, MetaMap (Aronson, 2001) to provide various biomedical information as categories. MetaMap extracts biomedical NEs from raw texts and matches them into semantic types of UMLS. Unified Medical Language System (UMLS) (Lindberg et al., 1993) is a thesaurus that provides the biomedical NEs and their semantic categories as an annotation. UMLS includes an amount of concept categories and a semantic network likes UMLS semantic type. Similar UMLS semantic types are grouped into UMLS semantic group. In this paper, we regard the annotation of biomedical NEs as UMLS semantic group. Table 1 shows UMLS semantic groups. UMLS semantic groups cover not only gene and protein but various sub-domains such as anatomy, procedure, and medical device. Biomedical NEs and their semantic types from MetaMap are usefully used in biomedical QA systems and biomedical topic modeling systems that require similarity of biomedical terms. MetaMap is a useful tool to analyze the biomedical text, however, there are several limitations (Zhang and Elhadad., 2013) because UMLS covers the huge knowledge and there are a lot of newly generated biomedical NEs in a real world. First, MetaMap extracts not only biomedical NEs but also common entities or even verbs that are not biomedical NEs clearly. Second, MetaMap does not resolve the ambiguity of UMLS semantic group types without context. That is, one entity can have several annotations. This limitation is 'ambiguity problem' in this paper. Finally, if some biomedical NE is not recorded in UMLS thesaurus, MetaMap cannot assign UMLS semantic group. We named this limitation 'out-of-vocabulary problem'. Thus, we present how to develop an effective biomedical NE recognition system by applying the advantages and overcoming the limitations of MetaMap.

We had been devised NE recognition system find the similarity of biomedical NEs in a query and biomedical NEs in candidate answer in biomedical QA system based on information retrieval (Lee et al., 2016). This QA system is entered for 2016 BioASQ challenge (Tsatsaronis et al., 2012).

2 Proposed Method

To overcome limitations of MetaMap, we propose a method to automatically construct a biomedical NE recognition data using a small amount of labeled data, a large amount of unlabeled data and MetaMap. Firstly, we develop a chunker learned by a small amount of biomedical training data annotated by the people. This chunker is used to generate the labeled training data for the self-training approach. The chunking results of unlabeled biomedical corpus become the inputs of MetaMap. Then the outputs of MetaMap, UMLS

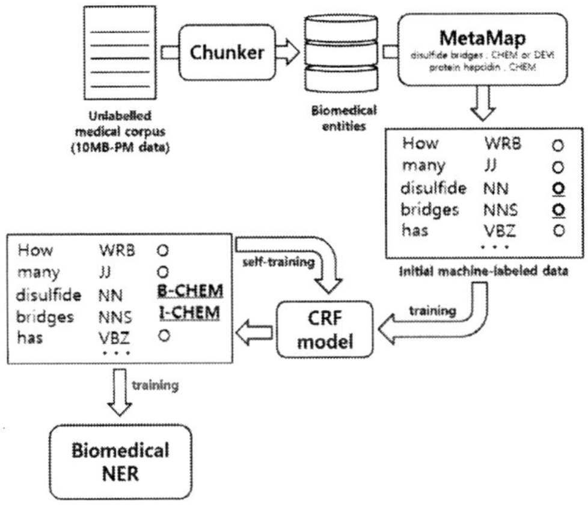

Figure 1: Overview of proposed method

semantic types, become match the UMLS semantic groups are used to make an initial machine-labeled data. We develop a biomedical NE recognition system with initial machine-labeled data and conditional random fields (CRF) classifier. The initial machine-labeled data has a form of semantic role labelling with an IOB2 format. This classifier is an initial model for self-training. Our proposed self-training process is described in Section 2.2. During self-training, this process is repeated, and then overcome the ambiguity problem and out–of–vocabulary problem.

Figure 1 shows the example of overcoming the ambiguity problem. In initial machine-labeled data, 'disulfide bridges' denoted by underline has a 'O' tag, but after the self-training process the entity, disulfide bridges, has a 'CHEM' tag.

2.1 Initial Machine-Labeled Data

In this section, we present the method for generating the initial machine-labeled data for self-training. We propose a semi-supervised approach using MetaMap, a small amount of labeled training data and a large amount of unlabeled data to generate a large amount of machine-labeled training data. The unlabeled data is randomly selected titles and abstracts from the PubMed biomedical articles. In this paper, we call the unlabeled data as a 10MB-PM data.

In order to generate training data, we first develop a chunker to overcome the problem that MetaMap extract several entities even if they are not biomedical NEs. The chunker is developed with a small amount of labeled data. The NE candidates of the 10MB-PM data are chunked by the chunker and then only the NE chunks are exploited as the input of MetaMap to label biomedical NEs.

We now explain how to create a large amount of initial machine-labeled data with the analysis results of MetaMap. NE chunks from the chunker are used as the input of MetaMap and then MetaMap analyses their semantic types. We mapped 133 UMLS semantic types to 15 UMLS semantic groups depanding on semilarity. The semantic groups are regarded as annotation of biomedical NEs. If MetaMap outputs only one semantic group type for a biomedical NE chunk, we assume that this semantic group type is a correct annotation of the NE chunk. In this case, each word of the NE chunk is labeled by B or I tag with UMLS group as annotation. For example, there is a NE chunk 'protein hepcidin' from 10MB-PM data. The output of MetaMap as semantic group type of 'protein hepcidin' is 'CHEM'. To generate automatically labeled data, we tag the 'B-CHEM' to 'protein' and 'I-CHEM' to 'hepcidin'. However, in some cases, MetaMap outputs several semantic groups or no group type for an input NE chunk. In these cases, the NE chunks are not considered as a biomedical NEs and their words are initially labeled by O tags. We try to recover them in order to generate a robust machine-labeled data through the self-training.

2.2 Self-training

The self-training approach is one of the semi-supervised learning. In Self-training, a classifier is trained with the manually annotated data. Then the unlabeled data is input the classifier. All or part of a result of the classifier is used as a training data.

Through a self-training procedure, we can overcome the ambiguity and out-of-vocabulary problems in machine-labeled data. The proposed self-training procedure performs the following steps in an iterative procedure. First, CRFs is trained using initial machine-labeled data, and then the sequential labelling results of the trained CRFs are compared the ones of the initial machine-labeled data as an answer. If the entity with O tag in the initial machine-labeled data are changed B or I tag by the trained CRFs model, the tags of this entity is replaced with the new B or I tag in new training data. This new training data is used as the input training data for the next self-training iteration. This iterative procedure is conducted until the performance of the classifier is converged. In each repeated step, new labeled biomedical NEs are added in the training data.

In case of biomedical NE chunk that has the ambiguity problem or out-of-vocabulary problem, we cannot make a decision to the categories of that NE chunks. Thus we annotate the O tag to that NE chunk. In other words, entities that have ambiguity UMLS semantic group or no UMLS semantic group cannot exist in automatically labeled data. However, their categories are recovered appropriate tag by proposed self-training. It is the main reason that the proposed NE recognition system showed high recall scores in our experiments.

For example, the word, 'drisapersen,' is biomedical NE of the drugs but this entity is not recorded in the UMLS thesaurus. After executing our self-training procedure, the word 'drisapersen' and its semantic group type, 'CHEM,' are analyzed as a correct biomedical NE; 'CHEM' is a chemical category as a semantic group type that includes drugs, protein, steroid, vitamin, and others.

3 Experiments

3.1 Experimental Settings

We constructed a manually annotated dataset that consists of 1,249 biomedical question/answer pairs from BioASQ 2015 and 2016. A half of the annotated data was used as a training data and the other data was used as a test data. The test dataset is composed of 624 question/answer pairs and 1,492 biomedical NEs. In test data, there are 1,492 biomedical NEs. The 10MB-PM data is organized by 7,629 PubMed articles that are arbitrary selected. To evaluate the quality of machine-labeled data, we evaluated biomedical NE recognition systems that are trained with the machine-labeled data of each self-training iteration with precision, recall, and f1-score.

3.2 Experimental Result and Evaluation

'MetaMap' in the first row is a model that is used MetaMap as biomedical NE recognition system. We input the raw text into MetaMap, and then evaluated the performance. An 'Initial model' is the model that is trained with initial machine-labeled data. The initial machine-labeled data is generated by applying chunker and MetaMap. A 'Second-iteration model' in the third row means self-training model with initial model. Row 4-6 are result of models that each iteration of self-training.

In Table 2, the initial model shows much-improved performance. The performance of MetaMap is much lower than the initial model. In particular, the precision score of MetaMap is much worse than recall score because it outputs common nouns and verbs as biomedical NEs. On the other hand, the chunker used in initial model is trained to extract only biomedical NEs with a small amount of manually annotated data. That is why the precision score of initial model is more improved than MetaMap.

To recover NE entities with ambiguity and out-of-vocabulary, the self-training procedure is developed in our biomedical NE recognition system. The performance changes of self-training according to the number of iteration times are shown in row 2 to row 6 in Table 2. The best performance was obtained in the third iteration. The performance of third ST model and fourth ST model is a lower than second ST model. That is conducting the too much self-training makes some decrease of performance because noises can be generated by recovering the wrong biomedical NEs. With the self-training method, we can increase the F1-score from 68.04% to 69.91%.

Model	Precision	Recall	F1-score
MetaMap	34.98%	58.8%	43.88%
Initial model	83.01%	57.64%	68.04%
Second iteration model	79.93%	60.32%	68.75%
Third iteration model	79.91%	62.13%	69.91%
Fourth iteration model	77.85%	59.58%	67.50%
Fifth iteration model	71.88%	49.87%	58.88%

Table 2: The performance changes according to our proposed method

4 Conclusion and Future Work

In this paper, we proposed the method for generating machine-labeled biomedical NE recognition data with the self-training method. Through various experiments, we verified the performances of the biomedical NE recognition system that trained with our proposed machine-labeled data. The final system outperformed MetaMap with 26.03%. In addition, the proposed method has more strong points. To generate a large amount of data, we only used a small amount of training data. Therefore the cost to generate a data for the biomedical NE recognition systems can be reduced. Since MetaMap as an open toolkit is used, developers can build up the biomedical NE recognition systems without expert's help in biomedical domains.

As a future work, we plan to apply deep neural network techniques to construct the biomedical NE recognition systems.

Acknowledgement

This research was supported by the MISP(Ministry of Science, ICT & Future Planning), Korea, under the National Program for Excellence in SW)(2015-0-00910) supervised by the IITP(Institute for Information & communications Technology Promotion)

References

Alan R. Aronson. "Effective mapping of biomedical text to the UMLS Metathesaurus: the MetaMap program." *Proceedings of the AMIA Symposium*. American Medical Informatics Association, 2001.

Jin-Dong Kim, Tomoko Ohta, Yuka Tateisi, and Jun'ichi Tsujii. "GENIA corpus—a semantically annotated corpus for bio-textmining." *Bioinformatics*, 19(1), 2003, i180-i182.

Hyeon-gu Lee, Minkyoung Kim, Harksoo Kim, Juae Kim, Sunjae Kwon, Jungyun Seo, Jungkyu Cho, and Yi-reun Kim. "KSAnswer: Question-answering System of Kangwon National University and Sogang University in the 2016 BioASQ Challenge." *ACL 2016*, 2016, pp.45-49.

Lishuang Li, Liuke Jin, Zhenchao Jiang, Dingxin Song, and Degen Huang. "Biomedical named entity recognition based on extended recurrent neural networks." *Bioinformatics and Biomedicine (BIBM), 2015 IEEE International Conference on*. IEEE, 2015.

Lishuang Li, Liuke Jin, Yuxin Jiang, and Degen Huang. "Recognizing Biomedical Named Entities Based on the Sentence Vector/Twin Word Embeddings Conditioned Bidirectional LSTM." *China National Conference on Chinese Computational Linguistics*. Springer International Publishing, 2016.

Donald A. Lindberg, Betsy L. Humphreys, and Alexa T. McCray. "The Unified Medical Language System." *IMIA Yearbook*, 1993, pp.281-291.

Leaman Robert, Chih-Hsuan Wei, and Zhiyong Lu. "tmChem: a high performance approach for chemical named entity recognition and normalization." *Journal of cheminformatics*, 7(1), 2015.

George Tsatsaronis Michael Schroeder, Georgios Paliouras Yannis Almirantis, Ion Androutsopoulos, Eric Gaussier, Patrick Gallinari Thierry Artieres, Michael R. Alvers Matthias Zschunke, and Axel-Cyrille Ngonga Ngomo. "BioASQ: A Challenge on Large-Scale Biomedical Semantic Indexing and Question Answering." *AAAI fall symposium: Information retrieval and knowledge discovery in biomedical text*, 2012.

Zhiqiang Zeng, Hua Shi, Yun Wu, and Zhiling Hong. "Survey of natural language processing techniques in bioinformatics." *Comp Math Methods Med 2015*, article 674296.

Shaodian Zhang, and Noémie Elhadad. "Unsupervised biomedical named entity recognition: Experiments with clinical and biological texts." *Journal of biomedical informatics*, 46(6), 2013, pp.1088-1098.

Enhancing Drug-Drug Interaction Classification with Corpus-level Feature and Classifier Ensemble

Jing-Cyun Tu
Yuan-Ze University, Taoyuan, Taiwan
st410634@gmail.com

Po-Ting Lai
National Tsing-Hua University, HsinChu, Taiwan
potinglai@gmail.com

Richard Tzong-Han Tsai*
National Central University, Taoyuan, Taiwan
thtsai@csie.ncu.edu.tw

Abstract

The study of drug-drug interaction (DDI) is important in the drug discovering. Both PubMed and DrugBank are rich resources to retrieve DDI information which is usually represented in plain text. Automatically extracting DDI pairs from text improves the quality of drug discovering. In this paper, we presented a study that focuses on the DDI classification. We normalized the drug names, and developed both sentence-level and corpus-level features for DDI classification. A classifier ensemble approach is used for the unbalance DDI labels problem. Our approach achieved an F-score of 65.4% on SemEval 2013 DDI test set. The experimental results also show the effects of proposed corpus-level features in the DDI task.

1 Introduction

Drug-drug interaction (DDI) is a situation that a drug modifies the effect of another drug, and the modified effect may be increased, decreased or new. For examples, if a patient takes two drugs and one increases the effect of another, an overdose may occur. In contrary, an under dosage may occur if the effect is decreased. Furthermore, the DDI may also cause the side effects. Therefore, the survey of DDI studies is important for improving the quality of drug discovering. Many drug-drug interactions are publicly available through PubMed or DrugBank (Law, et al., 2014). However, only a fraction of them is in a structured format such as DrugBank (Law, et al., 2014). Most DDIs are represented in unstructured plane text. Therefore, automatically extracting DDI form these texts is an important issue.

In 2013, SemEval (Segura-Bedmar, et al., 2013) sets this task as the one of its shared task challenge. Extracting DDI consists of two tasks: (1) drug name recognition (DNR) and (2) DDI classification. The named entity recognition (NER) is usually formulated as the sequence label problem and resolved by the Conditional Random Fields model (Campos, et al., 2013; Leaman, et al., 2015). The most important thing is to design and select proper features which capture the boundaries of the named entities. For DNR, several approaches (Björne, et al., 2013; Liu, et al., 2015; Rocktäschel, et al., 2013) have been proposed. For instance, Liu et.al (Liu, et al., 2015) considered selecting DNR features as a feature engineering problem, and their experiments combined several features. Their approach achieved an F-score of 79.36% in the DDIExtraction 2013 dataset (Segura-Bedmar, et al., 2013).

The second task is to classify the drug-drug pair in the sentence into one of advice, effect, mechanism, int (interaction) or negative labels. The advice label indicates that the drug-drug pair is recommended or advised to have the interaction. The effect label indicates that the DDI effect is described in the sentence. The mechanism label indicates that the DDI is described about Pharmacology which includes both pharmacodynamics and pharmacokinetics. The int label indicates that the physical interaction is stated without any other information. The negative label indicates that there is no interaction. For the second task, several Machine Learning (ML)-based approaches have been proposed. For an example, WBI-DDI (Thomas, et al., 2013) proposed a two-step strategy. They detect general drug-drug interactions regardless of subtype using the different machine-learning methods, and proposed an ensemble voting approach to ensemble these methods. Their approach achieved an F-score of

* Corresponding author

Proceedings of the International Workshop on Digital Disease Detection using Social Media 2017 (DDDSM-2017), pages 52–56, Taipei, Taiwan, November 27, 2017. ©2017 AFNLP

60.9%. The ML-based approaches usually suffered from bias number of the positive and negative DDI pairs. Only few of them have true interactions. To resolve this problem, FBK-irst (Chowdhury and Lavelli, 2013) proposed a multi-phase kernel-based approach. They consider the negative DDI sentence and pair as less informative sentence (LLS) and less informative instance (LLI). They design the rules and classifier to discard LLS and LLI. They proposed a hybrid kernel approach and several syntactic dependent features for DDI detection and classification. Their approach achieves an F-score of 65% on SemEval DDI 2013 test set (Segura-Bedmar, et al., 2013).

Despise many DDI classification approaches had been proposed, the approaches for DDI still can be further improved. For an example, since a drug can be represented in its branded name or generic name, the interaction describe in other sentence could not be directly used in other sentences without linking its different names. Therefore, the features used in current approaches usually focus on sentence-level and the information above the target DDI sentences, such as corpus-level features, were not referred. Iyer et.al. (Iyer, et al., 2013) proposed an annotation-based approach to learn DDI from the electronic medical records (EMR). Since the EMR has rich temporal information such as section times, they annotate temporal relationship between the drugs and event and calculate the odds ratio (OR) of the drug-drug pair with events to only one drug with the event. Their experimental results show the effect of odds ratio in learning DDI pairs.

In this paper, we present a study that focuses on the second task. First, we proposed a ML-based approach which includes the basic words, Part-of-speech, syntactic and template features as our baseline. Second, we deal with the drug various names and proposed the corpus-level features by calculating the odds ratios of the drugs matched our automatically generated DDI template which is inspired by Iyer et.al.'s approach (Iyer, et al., 2013). Third, to tackle the bias labels in DDI corpus, we used a classifier ensemble approach with voting strategy. The experiments are in the SemEval DDI 2013 dataset (Segura-Bedmar, et al., 2013). Our proposed approach achieved an F-score of 65.4%, which outperforms both WBI-DDI and FBK-irst's approaches.

2 Method

The proposed DDI classification approach consists of four main steps. The first is *Drug Name Normalization*, which used RxNorm (Nelson, et al., 2011) to normalize drug synonyms in order calculate odds ratio more accurately. Following is the *Odds Ratio* step, in which we calculate the odds ratio of drug-drug pair matched DDI templates to only one drug matched. Next, *Features for Classification* presents the DDI classification features. Lastly, the *Classifier Ensemble* divides positive and negative training data into equal size, and training five classifiers in the different sets, then used a voting strategy to ensemble classification results.

2.1 Drug Name Normalization

A drug might be represented as its generic name or branded name in the text. Here we refer them as drug synonyms. To normalize the synonyms can make the calculation of odds ratio more accurately. RxNorm is a tool developed by National Library of Medicine (NIH). It contains the normalized drug names and links them to many drug vocabularies which are commonly used in pharmacy management and drug interaction software. RxNorm can links the drug names between different systems which do not use the same software and vocabulary. Before calculating the odds ratio, we will use RxNorm to normalize the drug name d into its generic name g. If the d cannot be normalized to any generic name, then we will use d as its normalized name.

2.2 Odds Ratio

The odds is the ratio r of the probability p_1 that the event of interest occurs to the probability p_2 that it does not occur. This is often estimated by the ratio of the number of times t_1 that the event of interest occurs to the number of times t_2 that it does not. In this paper, the odds ratio refers to the ratio or of the odds r_1 that the drug d_1 interacts with the drug d_2 to the odds r_2 that d_1 or d_2 interacts with the other drugs. For example, the odds r_1 that a drug d_1 interacts with the drug d_2 is 4 and the odds r_2 that d_1 or d_2 interacts with the other drugs is 2. The odds ratio or of d_1 and d_2 will be 4/2 = 2. The higher or indicates the higher odds that d_1 and d_2 have interaction than they interact with the other drugs. While calculating or, whether d_1 interacts with d_2 is obtained by the DDI templates which we will introduce in section 2.3.2.

2.3 Features for Classification

Our classifier uses basic, template and odds ratio

features. The basic and template features utilized the immediate context of the drugs pair as features, whereas odds ratio features used the corpus-level information.

2.3.1 Basic Features

The basic features comprised words, Part-of-speech (POS) and syntactic features. There are two sets of word features used in our system, each with a different feature label. Inter-Drugs *n*-grams set includes all word unigrams and bigrams located between drugs. If none is present, the feature is given a *"NULL"* value. Surrounding Words set includes the two words before the first drug and the two after the second drug. If there are no words before or after both NEs, a *"NULL"* value is set. All words are treated as bag-of-words. That is, the order of these words is not considered. Similarly, the unigrams of POS tags between drugs are also used as POS features. We also parse each sentence with a full-sentence syntactic parser (Roark, et al., 2006) to generate its full parse tree. We use the syntactic path through the parse tree from the drug d_1 to the drug d_2 as a feature.

2.3.2 Template Features

Our template generation (TG) algorithm, which extracts word patterns for drugs pairs using Smith and Waterman's local alignment algorithm (Smith and Waterman, 1981). Firstly, we pair all sentences containing positive relations. The sentence pairs are then aligned word-by-word and a pattern satisfying the alignment result is created. Each slot in the template is given by the corresponding constraint information expressed in the form of a word (e.g. *"associated"*). If two aligned sentences have nothing in common for a given slot, the TG algorithm puts a wildcard in the position. The complete TG algorithm is described with pseudo code in the Algorithm. The similarity function used to compare the similarity of two tokens in local algorithm is defined as:

$$Sim(x, y) = \max\begin{cases} \mathbf{1}, & \textbf{if } x = y \\ \mathbf{0}, & \textbf{otherwise} \end{cases}$$

where x and y are tokens in sentences s_i and s_j, respectively. The similarity of two sentences is calculated by the local algorithm on the basis of this token-level similarity function.

Template Generation Algorithm

```
INPUT: A set of sentences S = {s_1, ..., s_k}
T = {};
for s_i in s_1 to s_{k-1}
    for s_j in s_{i+1} to s_k
        if the similarity of s_i and s_j above the threshold
        then generate template t from s_i and s_j
            T <- t;
    end;
end;
return T
OUTPUT: A set of templates T = {t_1, ..., t_k}
```

2.3.3 Odds Ratio Features

The odds ratio is the ratio of one odds to another, and it is larger than zero. In our experiment, we use different thresholds as odd ratio features include 1.0, 1.5, 2.0 and 2.5. The real number of odds ratio is also used as one of the odds ratio features.

2.4 Classifier Ensemble

The amount of negative DDI pairs is higher than the positive ones in both DDI corpus and real world. The support vector machine model (Chang and Lin, 2011) used in our experiment is suffered from this problem. To tackle this problem, we proposed a classifier ensemble approach to training our classifiers. Firstly, we randomly divide the negative data into five unique subsets, since the ratio of the positive pairs to the negative pairs is approximate 5 in the experimental training corpus. Secondly, we construct five training datasets that each contains all positive data and one negative subset. Thirdly, we train five base classifiers with SVM. Here we use the Gaussian kernel. Once the classifiers are constructed, new DDI pairs are classified by the classifiers, and their results are aggregated to form the final ensemble decision output. The vote method is used in this paper. Given classifiers C_i, $i = 1, 2, \ldots, N_C$, and DDI labels L_j , $j = 1, 2, \ldots, N_L$, where N_C is the ensemble size and N_L is the number of DDI labels. The final aggregated decision is the winning classifier that has the highest votes across all classifiers. If any tie situation existed, the label with the highest predicted value will be assigned.

3 Experiments

To evaluate our approach, the SemEval 2013 DDI corpus is used. Table 1 shows the number of the DDI categories annotated in the corpus. The most common type was negative pairs in both training and test set. Here, we first compare the performance achieved by baseline features (basic + template features) to the baseline + odds ratio (OR) features. In Table 2, we can see that OR features improve the baseline's performance by an F-score 11.9%. Our approach performs better than FBK-irst and WBI-DDI, because our OR features are effective. In Table 3, we list the F-score for each category of DDI. We observe that the F-scores for advice and mechanism are comparatively high. This is possibly because they have some specific keywords in both categories. However, although effect is the second most frequent category, it does not have a high F-score. We think this discrepancy is due to the fact that the descriptions of DDI effects are commonly presented more flexible. Int's performance is comparatively higher than the other two systems since the OR features are effective while the training set is very small.

Type		Training set	Test set
#Documents		456	116
#Sentence		2915	341
#Positive pairs	**Advice**	658	160
	Effect	1243	292
	Mechanism	1004	253
	Int	168	10
	Total	3073	715
#Negative pairs		17905	4312
#Total pair		20978	5027

Table 1: The statistic of DDI dataset

Configuration	P(%)	R(%)	F(%)
Baseline	50.4	57.0	53.4
WBI-DDI	64.2	57.9	60.9
FBK-irst	65.0	66.0	65.0
Baseline + OR	64.0	66.7	**65.3**

Table 2: The DDI classification performances on the test set

Category	Baseline + OR	FBK-irst	WBI-DDI
Advice	**69.5**	69.2	63.2
Effect	62.3	**62.8**	61.0
Mechanism	**68.2**	67.9	61.8
INT	**60.0**	54.7	51.0
Overall	**65.3**	65.0	60.9

Table 3. The F-scores of individual DDI categories on the test set

4 Conclusion

In this paper, we present a classifier ensemble approach for drug-drug interaction classification. We developed the sentence-level features for the classification. To encode corpus-level odds ratio features, we used the RxNorm to normalize the drug names. Our ensemble classifier achieves an F-score of 65.4% on SemEval 2013 DDI test set. The results underscore the effect of corpus-level features in classifying the drug-drug interaction.

Reference

Björne, J., Kaewphan, S. and Salakoski, T. (2013) UTurku: Drug Named Entity Recognition and Drug-Drug Interaction Extraction Using SVM Classification and Domain Knowledge. *Second Joint Conference on Lexical and Computational Semantics (*SEM), Volume 2: Proceedings of the Seventh International Workshop on Semantic Evaluation (SemEval 2013).* Association for Computational Linguistics, pp. 651-659.

Campos, D., Matos, S. and Oliveira, J.L. (2013) Gimli: open source and high-performance biomedical name recognition, *BMC Bioinformatics*, 14, 54.

Chang, C.-C. and Lin, C.-J. (2011) LIBSVM: A library for support vector machines, *ACM Trans. Intell. Syst. Technol.*, 2, 1-27.

Chowdhury, M.M.F. and Lavelli, A. (2013) FBK-irst : A Multi-Phase Kernel Based Approach for Drug-Drug Interaction Detection and Classification that Exploits Linguistic Information. *Second Joint Conference on Lexical and Computational Semantics (*SEM), Volume 2: Proceedings of the Seventh International Workshop on Semantic Evaluation (SemEval 2013).* Association for Computational Linguistics, pp. 351-355.

Iyer, S.V., *et al.* (2013) Learning Signals of Adverse Drug-Drug Interactions from the Unstructured Text of Electronic Health Records, *AMIA Summits on Translational Science Proceedings*, 2013, 98-98.

Law, V., *et al.* (2014) DrugBank 4.0: shedding new light on drug metabolism, *Nucleic*

Acids Research, 42, D1091-D1097.

Leaman, R., Wei, C.-H. and Lu, Z. (2015) tmChem: a high performance approach for chemical named entity recognition and normalization, *Journal of Cheminformatics*, 7, S3.

Liu, S., *et al.* (2015) Feature Engineering for Drug Name Recognition in Biomedical Texts: Feature Conjunction and Feature Selection, *Computational and Mathematical Methods in Medicine*, 2015, 9.

Nelson, S.J., *et al.* (2011) Normalized names for clinical drugs: RxNorm at 6 years, *Journal of the American Medical Informatics Association : JAMIA*, 18, 441-448.

Roark, B., *et al.* (2006) SParseval: Evaluation metrics for parsing speech, *Proc. LREC*.

Rocktäschel, T., *et al.* (2013) WBI-NER: The impact of domain-specific features on the performance of identifying and classifying mentions of drugs. *Second Joint Conference on Lexical and Computational Semantics (*SEM), Volume 2: Proceedings of the Seventh International Workshop on Semantic Evaluation (SemEval 2013).* Association for Computational Linguistics, pp. 356-363.

Segura-Bedmar, I., Martínez, P. and Herrero Zazo, M. (2013) SemEval-2013 Task 9 : Extraction of Drug-Drug Interactions from Biomedical Texts (DDIExtraction 2013). *Second Joint Conference on Lexical and Computational Semantics (*SEM), Volume 2: Proceedings of the Seventh International Workshop on Semantic Evaluation (SemEval 2013).* Association for Computational Linguistics, pp. 341-350.

Smith, T.F. and Waterman, M.S. (1981) Identification of common molecular subsequences, *Journal of Molecular Biology*, 147, 195-197.

Thomas, P., *et al.* (2013) WBI-DDI: Drug-Drug Interaction Extraction using Majority Voting. *Second Joint Conference on Lexical and Computational Semantics (*SEM), Volume 2: Proceedings of the Seventh International Workshop on Semantic Evaluation (SemEval 2013).* Association for Computational Linguistics, pp. 628-635.

Chemical-Induced Disease Detection Using Invariance-based Pattern Learning Model

Neha Warikoo[123], Yung-Chun Chang[4] and Wen-Lian Hsu[3]*

[1]Institute of Biomedical Informatics, National Yang-Ming University, Taipei, 112, Taiwan
[2]Bioinformatics Program, Taiwan International Graduate Program, Institute of Information Science, Academia Sinica, Taipei 115, Taiwan
[3]Institute of Information Science, Academia Sinica, Taipei 115 Taiwan
[4]Graduate Institute of Data Science, Taipei Medical University, Taipei 106, Taiwan

Abstract

In this work, we introduce a novel feature engineering approach named "algebraic invariance" to identify discriminative patterns for learning relation pair features for the chemical-disease relation (CDR) task of BioCreative V. Our method exploits the existing structural similarity of the key concepts of relation descriptions from the CDR corpus to generate robust linguistic patterns for SVM tree kernel-based learning. Preprocessing of the training data classifies the entity pairs as either related or unrelated to build instance types for both inter-sentential and intra-sentential scenarios. An invariant function is proposed to process and optimally cluster similar patterns for both positive and negative instances. The learning model for CDR pairs is based on the SVM tree kernel approach, which generates feature trees and vectors and is modeled on suitable invariance based patterns, bringing brevity, precision and context to the identifier features. Results demonstrate that our method outperformed compared approaches, achieved a high recall rate of 85.08%, and averaged an F_1-score of 54.34% without the use of any additional knowledge bases.

1 Introduction

Causality or association determination between target entities, especially those involved in diseases, has quickly become the topic of interest within the area of biomedical text mining. Such studies have created a large number of information pools that enables clinicians to make diagnoses more effectively. A pertinent example is the prediction of chemical-disease interactions based on biomedical text, which if used to its fullest potential can revolutionize the way precision medicine and drug testing is conducted. The idea is to preemptively identify any associations between a drug and subsequent physiological responses for subjects accepting treatment for a disease (Wei et al. 2015). Most of the physiological responses emerge as secondary disease symptoms and often as adverse drug reactions. If studied in appropriate context, these events may contain information of unwanted damages to the patients. Any side effects or adverse drug reactions can be avoided for patients participating in clinical trials if similar trials have had invoked deleterious responses in its participants, which can be heuristically implied by textual and statistical evidence presented in scientific publications and other approved research materials.

Recently, BioCreative V introduced the task of chemical-induced disease (CID) relation extraction from PubMed abstracts, focusing on identifying chemical and disease entities acting in a "cause and effect" mannerism in a binary association. We have adapted the same task guidelines to shape our objective of identifying chemical-induced diseases via pattern-based learning. Our approach for the CID task attempts to capture the commonalty in structured patterns used to describe such relations. Corresponding positive and negatives instances from abstracts are processed as vector representations converged into signature patterns that can be accessorized as identifiers for the nature of the relationship. The generated patterns are then learned by using the convolution tree kernel (CTK) to classify potential entity pairs.

Unlike other relation extraction tasks, the vague context of associating entities in the sentences generated by intra-sentential and inter-sentential association pairs increases the complexity of this dataset. In an intra-sentential scenario, the chemical-induced drug response is explicitly given within a sentence. An example is the relation between "cocaine" and "myocardial infrac-

* Corresponding author

Proceedings of the International Workshop on Digital Disease Detection using Social Media 2017 (DDDSM-2017), pages 57–64,
Taipei, Taiwan, November 27, 2017. ©2017 AFNLP

tion and bundle branch block" shown in Figure 1 (a). As for inter-sentential cases, the association statements can span across several sentences. Figure 1 (b) indicates the specific effects of audiovisual toxicity caused by "desferrioxamine" can only be established by parsing multiple statements describing the secondary links identified through the perception of "audiovisual defects".

(a): Intra-sentential

Electrocardiographic evidence of myocardial injury in psychiatrically hospitalized *cocaine* abusers...... Eleven of the *cocaine* abusers and none of the controls had ECG evidence of significant myocardial injury defined as *myocardial infarction*, ischemia, and *bundle branch block*.

(b): Inter-sentential

Ocular and auditory toxicity in hemodialyzed patients receiving *desferrioxamine*. During an 18-month period of study 41 hemodialyzed patients receiving *desferrioxamine* (10-40 mg/kg BW/3 times weekly) for the first time were monitored for detection of audiovisual toxicity....... Visual toxicity was of retinal origin and was characterized by a tritan-type dyschromatopsy, sometimes associated with a loss of visual acuity and *pigmentary retinal deposits*. Auditory toxicity was characterized by a mid- to high-frequency neurosensorial hearing loss and the lesion was of the cochlear type...... Please make both abstracts as a figure.

Figure 1: Intra-sentential and inter-sentential cases from the corpus.

To resolve this complexity, we developed a preprocessing module to identify sentences based on permutations of all possible entities. In addition, linguistic patterns were learned from biomedical literatures based on the concept of Algebraic Invariant. These patterns are provided to SVM based on convolution tree kernel as features for supervised learning. Depending on the characteristics captured by the patterns, the classifier aims to differentiate instances involving related and unrelated entity pairs.

2 Related Work

Since its inception, multiple learning approaches were employed with and without Knowledge Base (KB) to simplify the CID task. Zhou et al. (2015) used a shortest dependency tree-based method for relation extraction in the CDR corpus. They experimented with flattened features, structured features, and structured phrases and reported a F_1-score of 55.05% with a combination of all of the features. The approach of Pons et al. (2015) for the same task is based on their feature set established on a prior graph database for chemical-disease interaction along with separate sets of statistical and lexical features. Over a dozen lexical and dependency path based features were exploited by Gu et al. (2015) to demonstrate the effectiveness of intra-sentential and inter-sentential level classification using a Maximum Entropy model. Xu et al. (2015) utilized a knowledge base-targeted method in learning the relation patterns. In addition, they also employed context-based features along with some auxiliary features to short list the number of relations for sentence level and ultimately document level classifier. Le et al. (2015) applied a pipeline model based on co-reference resolution and intra-sentential relations. Based on the entity pairs recognized by the model, token dependent features, n-gram word features and graph-based features SVM classifiers were used for relation identification. Chemical-disease relations identified in the CTD[1] database were incorporated in lexical feature vectors by Alam et al. (2015) to add higher confidence value to significant features based on their collective mentions in the database. Moreover, Zhou et al. (2016) used variants of the neural network method to obtain performances ranging from 47.2 with a convolution neural network model to 61.3 with a hybrid model of tree-kernel based SVM, LSTM, and a post-processing module. As an extension of the neural network approach for this task, Gu et al. (2017) introduced another model based on their previous effort (Gu et al. 2015) in which they used ME to determine intra-sentential relations and a convolution neural network model for inter-sentential relation recognition. A post-processing module that removes redundancies and adjusts hypernyms was implemented to enhance the model.

Our model is KB independent with a SVM tree kernel learning method. It focuses on customizing the context of the learning tree to application relevance through our novel algebraic invariant pattern generation approach.

3 Method

The task of CID identification mandates pre-annotation of chemical and disease entities throughout the text. The organizers have used manual annotation along with *tmChem* (Leaman et al. 2015) and *DNorm* (Leaman et al. 2013) for chemical and disease term identification. In order

[1] https://toxnet.nlm.nih.gov/newtoxnet/ctd.htm

to focus on relation extraction, we decided to use the pre-annotations given in the training, development, and test datasets for generating possible relation entity pairs in each respective set. To develop a classifier for recognizing related entity pairs, we divided our pattern learning effort into three different stages. The first stage is the preprocessing of biomedical text followed by candidate sentence selection. With the help of these candidate sentences, relevant context based patterns are exhumed from the original text. Values based on these patterns are used as coefficients variables in invariant polynomial function to cluster similar ranking patterns. Similar ranking patterns are aligned and restructured into a more generic form. Each of these patterns is used to generate feature file for SVM based tree kernel, in which everything except regional matches to context-based patterns are pruned. SVM classifier predicts the corresponding labels for the hence generated candidate instance based trees to determine the relation between the entity pairs. Each stage is illustrated in details in the subsequent sections.

3.1 Candidate Instance Generation

The abstract data in its initial form contains multiple entities associated with either intra-sentential or inter-sentential relations, thereby increasing the difficulty of this task. Moreover, other existing sentences may become noises as they do not corelate or attribute in any form in determining entity pair relations. Candidate Instance Generation entails screening for relation-oriented sentences, which are referred to as "Instances" henceforth. Prior to candidate instance generation, we proceeded with generic tasks of natural text preprocessing via Sentence Detection (Apache Open NLP)[2], Entity Class Labeling (In-built Module), and part-of-speech (POS) tagging (Genia Tagger)[3]. Moreover, we resolved duplicate adjacency entity labels (In-built Module), which are often observed in biomedical literature. For example, although "plasma renin activity (PRA)" is annotated with two separate labels "plasma renin activity" and "(PRA)", but they both correspond to the same bio-entity as the bracketed acronym mentioned in adjacency is a duplicate label. Resolving such duplicates optimizes the pair-based instance generation task.

We choose to generate candidate instances from POS tag-labeled sentences since they are more appropriate in depicting the skeletal similarity of relation expressions in contrast to natural text. Therefore, following the preprocessing, the POS-tagged data was drafted into candidate instances based on entity pairs (one chemical and one disease mention per sentence per pairwise iteration) relabeling to indicate the primary Chemical and Disease pair. The verb implying the relation (proximal verb) was also assigned a prominent identifier as shown in Figure 2.

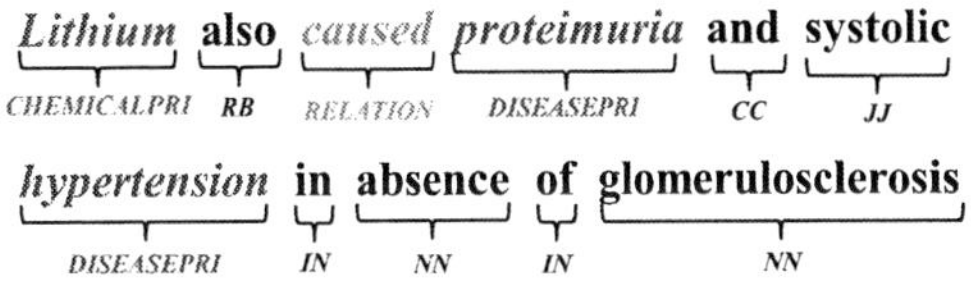

Figure 2: Candidate sentence tagging.

There can be more than one entity pair relations within a sentence. Therefore, for each pair set, a duplicate instance of the sentence highlighting the relevant pair is generated. Other than key entity pairs, we also identified and annotated the proximal verb with a third term "Relation". It entails a non-basal form verb nearest to the current entity pair set. The rationale of using this verb form is that in most sentences describing bio-entity relations, causal relations are asserted in a smaller frame within the sentence. Even in complex sentences, subject and the acted object are often linked by non-basal form verbs in close vicinity to the actors. Given the related entity pairs in the training data, positive and negative instances are generated and later processed by the successive feature-engineering module.

3.2 Invariance-based Feature Engineering

In our approach, we propose that different candidate instances show similarity in subject inference even if they are structurally diverse when relevant contexts are provided as reference points. There are multiple ways to communicate the same idea in a language, whether by direct implication or at times with additional context or compound references. However, in each of these cases, the skeleton of some reference points stays the same across different sentence structures. Our idea is to demonstrate the invariance or lack of change in the nature of such descriptive sections from the

[2] http://opennlp.sourceforge.net/models-1.5/en-sent.bin

[3] http://www.nactem.ac.uk/tsujii/GENIA/tagger/geniatagger-3.0.2.tar.gz

text, and exploit this characteristic in generating more robust features while limiting the degree of evaluation function.

The idea is heavily drawn on Algebraic Invariance to show that two separate sentences are similar in their inferential meaning if their invariant function does not vary. Such a function can be represented as follows:

$$I(q_{n0}\cdots q_{0n}) \equiv \Delta^{W} * I(p_{n0}\cdots p_{0n}) \qquad (1)$$

where *I(q)* and *I(p)* indicate the invariant function , Δ is the determinant of the representational polynomial undergone transformation, and *W* is the invariant weight. Any object/element can be represented in the Euclidean system using a polynomial function $P(x,y) = \sum p_{ij}x^i y^j$. Upon transformation "*T*", the same polynomial can be represented by another polynomial $Q(u,v) = \sum q_{ij}u^i v^j$, bound in relation *(u,v) = T(x,y)* with original form.

In order to restructure the invariance concept in a natural text paradigm, we used an assumed homogenous polynomial function based on three key referential groups viz. Entity1 (chemical), Relation (proximal verb), and Entity2 (disease) to project every instance in the Euclidian space. Since our primary goal is to identify chemical-induced diseases, we limited our function to a second order polynomial based on each variable set as given below:

$$P(x,y) = p_{20}x^2 + p_{11}x^1y^1 + p_{02}y^2 \qquad (2)$$

where *x* and *y* are representational binary association variables indicative of the "Entity1~Relation" and "Entity2~Relation" set, respectively. p_{20}, p_{11}, and p_{02} are coefficients of the representative polynomial evaluated by the maximum value from a five-frame adjacency matrix vector for each of the corresponding variable pairs. Our algorithm treats each candidate instance polynomial as a transformed version of all other instance polynomials. According to the concept of invariance, if the invariant functional of the current candidate polynomial is equal to the invariant functional of other instance polynomials, then the current instance is considered similar to each of those instances, thereby reducing the dimensionality of screening space for pattern generation and keeping context-specific similarities. In order to determine the invariant function, we assume rotation ($\phi = 0$) as transformation for our polynomial to calculate the corresponding invariant function for the given second order polynomial (Keren (1994)). The equation for calculating invariant polynomial in the assumed case is given below:

$$I(q_{no}\cdots q_{On}) \stackrel{\text{def}}{=} I(p_{no}\cdots p_{On}) = \left[p_{20}^2 + \left(\frac{p_{11}^2}{2}\right) + p_{02}^2\right] \qquad (3)$$

where *I(q)* and *I(p)* are the invariant functions for the transformed instance polynomial *Q(u,v)* and original instance polynomial *P(x,y)*, respectively. p_{20}, p_{11}, and p_{02} are the coefficients of the original polynomial function *P(x,y)*. Every candidate instance is screened for each of the three key referential groups as shown by candidate instances 1 and 2 in Figure 3, in which each underlined portion conforms a group of context patterns. Based upon their polynomial correspondence, the two candidate instances can be represented on coordinate space as demonstrated in Figure 4. The instances are also construed as proximal or non-proximal in structure depending upon the invariant scores. If they are similar, a generic context pattern can be obtained from both of them through alignment for each group.

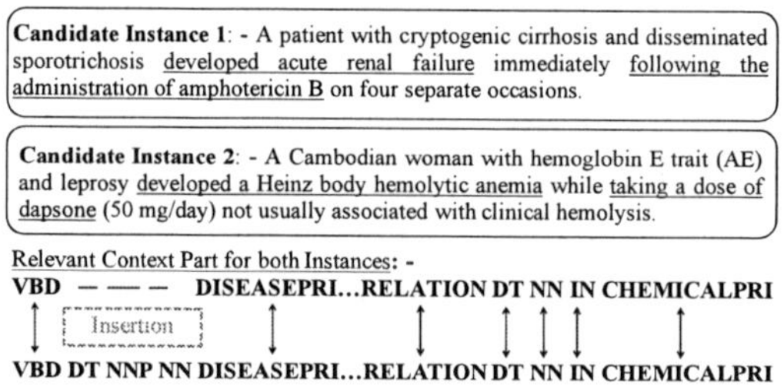

Figure 3: Context identification and prospective alignment of candidate instances.

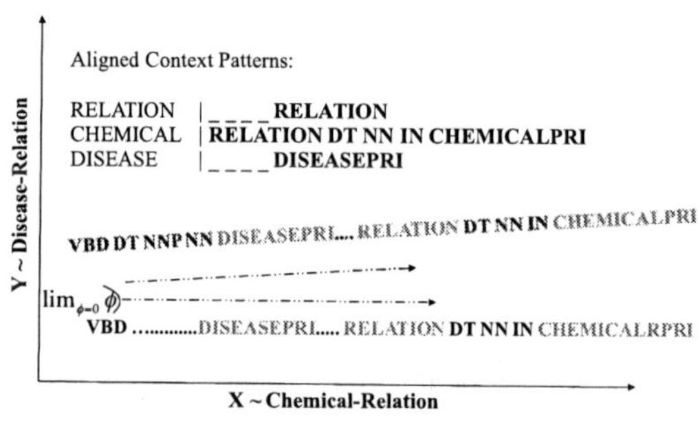

Figure 4: Vector representation of candidate instances on coordinate space.

For every referential group, 5 POS-tagged contextual frames with a range of 5 are generated by shifting the window frame iteratively over the instance, moving group index from 1 through 5. Then for each frame size, an adjacency matrix is generated per referential group by matching identical context patterns across instances to provide a statistical significance value for every instance as displayed in Figure 5. In addition to the repetitive count of contextual frames, each frame is individually scored to evaluate its significance. The context is scored using n-gram probabilistic model where n is the index of the referential entity group.

Since the index for reference group varies as per the frame being used, we have slightly modified the formula to accommodate the significance of whole patterns over the sub-patterns in the equation below. The modified formula takes into account all of the variant n-gram patterns both succeeded and preceded by the current referential group context. In this manner, it is able to attribute a more accurate representational value of the particular pattern from the entire context sample space.

$$\rho_{e_c k} = \begin{cases} \left(\dfrac{\sum P(x_0 \cdots x_{e_c})}{\sum P(x_0 \cdots x_{e_c - 1})}\right) + \left(\dfrac{\sum P(x_0 \cdots x_n)}{\sum P(x_0 \cdots x_{e_c})}\right) \\ \forall e_c < 5, n = 5 \\ \left(\dfrac{\sum P(x_0 \cdots x_{e_c})}{\sum P(x_0 \cdots x_{e_c - 1})}\right) + \delta_v \approx 0.0000000001 \\ \forall e_c = 5, n = 5 \end{cases} \quad (4)$$

where e_c is the index of the current referential group and n is the total size of frame. $\rho_{e_c k}$ is the score for each cell with frame size e_c and candidate instance k. $\sum P(x_0 \ldots x_n)$ is the number of times the current extracted POS frame of size 5 has occurred across all of the contexts generated from all instances. δ_v indicates the fringe value used in case the referential group has a terminal index. It is introduced to avoid attributing excess weight for standard n-gram patterns.

As indicated in Figure 5, since the variables in our polynomial equation (2) are based on binary association between entities, therefore the scores generated for each referential group are summed up with their corresponding pair variable score from the equation to evaluate the conjugate coefficient. Corresponding coefficient values from the homogenous representation equation (2) are substituted in equation (3) to obtain the invariant

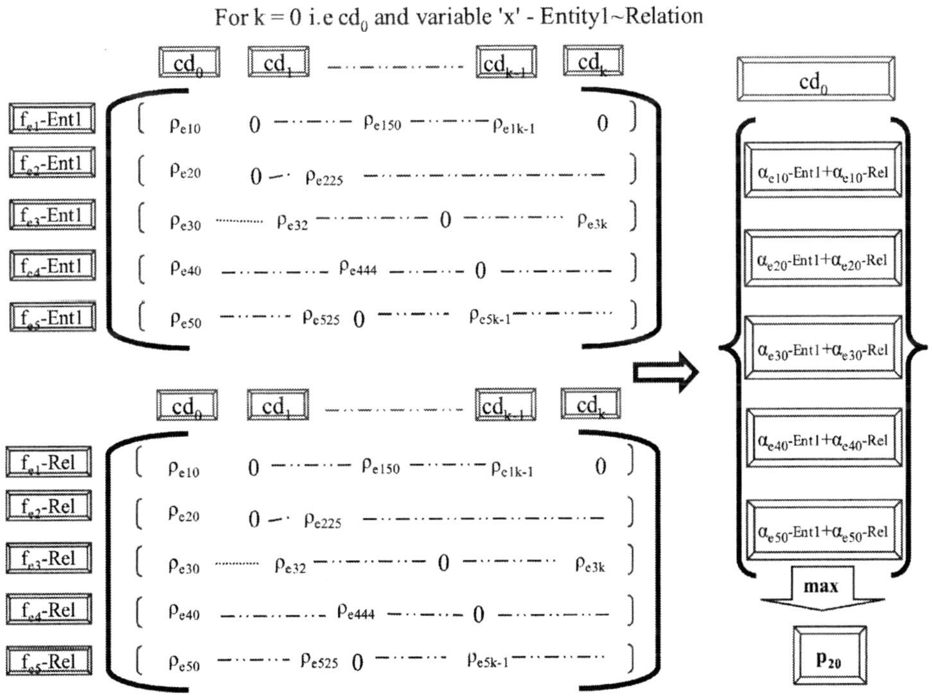

Figure 5: Adjacency matrix for calculation of representational polynomial coefficient

function score $I(p)_k$ in which k is the current candidate instance ID. The instances are then ranked in the descending order based on the calculated scores. According to equation (1) (set Δ=1.00 and W~1), each candidate instance is compared with its successor. If the approximation of values is similar, then the instances are considered as structurally similar and clustered together to form a feature attribute for classification. Otherwise, they are diversified into different pattern groups as illustrated in Figure 6. The clustered instances were used in pattern generation. Individual alignments were performed between instances for each of the referential groups (i.e. "Entity1-Chemical", "Relation-Proximal Verb", and "Entity2-Disease") to generate a triple context set-based pattern. The alignment is based on the highest scoring path obtained from the substitution matrix delivered by the recurrence relation:

$$sim(i,j) = \begin{cases} sim(i,j-1) + \\ \lambda(\_,j) \approx -2 \\ sim(i-1,j-1) + \\ \lambda(i,j) \approx \begin{vmatrix} 1\,\forall\, i = j \\ -1\,\forall\, i \neq j \end{vmatrix} \\ sim(i-1,j) + \\ \lambda(i,\_) \approx -2 \end{cases} \qquad (5)$$

where $sim(i,j)$ is the similarity score of the ith row and j^{th} column of the substitution matrix. $\lambda\,(i,j)$ indicates the penalty function scoring insertion, deletion, match or mismatch depending on the token comparison of respective indexes.

3.3 Tree Kernel Induced Learning

The stringent context patterns retrieved from invariance functions are mapped against the candidate instances, and the optimal match of each case is selected to define a feature tree for learning. Parse tree is generated using the Stanford parser (Chen and Manning 2014; Socher et al. 2013) and the selected context-based pattern determines which leaf nodes are to be pruned to refine the context of the tree. The tree is decorated through highlighting the instances with CID by prefixing a node for such positive instances. Along with the parse tree, a feature vector corresponding to each candidate instance is also maintained to examine the similarity of phrase structures (both simple and complex). Each phrase structure is characterized with an "ID", and the feature vector maintains the count of corresponding phrase structures per instance. A combination of the parse tree and feature vector is used in developing and testing the model. To classify the phrase structures according to the similarity index, Convolution Tree Kernel is employed to compare the substructures across parsed instances. SVM-Light-TK-1.5[4] toolkit was used in both the learning and classification modules (Moschitti 2004, 2006).

Algorithm 1: Invariance Pattern Generation

INPUT:
context$P$: $P_{Relation|Chemical|Disease}(x_0 \ldots x_n)_k$ triplet pattern for all candidate instances
ordered$I(P)$: Invariant functional score $I(P)_k$ for all candidate instances in descending order
BEGIN

```
set seedI(P) = orderedI(P)_0
set seedP = contextP_0
FOR k=0 : size(orderedI(P))
  currI(P) = orderedI(P)_k
  currP = contextP_k
  invarQuotient = ( seedI(P)/ currI(P))
  IF invarQuotient == 1.0
    reset seedP = align seedP with currP
    remove( orderedI(P)_k) & k = k-1| k!= 0
  ELSE
   IF seedP exists in InvariancePatterns
     remove( orderedI(P)_k) & k = k-1
   ELSE
     add(seedP) to InvariancePatterns
   seedI(P) = currI(P)
   seedP = currP
END FOR
add( seedP) to InvariancePatterns
```

OUTPUT: InvariancePatterns
END

Figure 6: Algorithm for Invariance Based Pattern Identification.

4 Experiments

4.1 Experiment Setup

We chose to adapt the CDR corpus released for BioCreative V – Track 2 to evaluate our method. The corpus comprises of 1500 PubMed abstracts in total, out of which 1400 abstracts were selected from the CTD-Pfizer collaboration corpus, with the remaining ones as new curations. The

[4] http://disi.unitn.it/moschitti/TK1.5-software/download.html

abstracts were equally distributed among the training, development, and test sets. Chemical and disease mentions were annotated and normalized to the corresponding MESH IDs (Li et al. 2016). Known chemical induced disease relations, determined from both the title and abstract text, were appended with each document ID. We did not conduct additional Named Entity Recognition (NER), and simply performed our analysis on the entities predefined in the dataset. Statistics on the entities and relation pairs within the corpus is displayed in Table 1. We evaluated the performance of relation detection in terms of the precision, recall, and the F_1-score. The F_1-score is the harmonic mean of the precision and recall, and is often selected to determine the overall effectiveness of a system.

Dataset	#Chemical	#Disease	#Relation
Train (500)	4182	5203	1038
Dev. (500)	4244	5347	1012
Test (500)	4424	5385	1066

Table 1: CDR Corpus Statistics

4.2 Results and Discussion

The performance of our method was compared with different approaches used for CID detection. Systems developed by Xu et al. (2015), Alam et al. (2015), and Pons et al. (2015), (Table 2) were based on using external KBs for relation pair identification. Xu et al. (2015) coupled the relation pair information from CTD, MEDI, and SIDER along with context-based features to optimize the learning and obtained F_1-score of 57.03%. Alam et al. (2015) developed a binary feature vector set model based on various characteristics exhibited by the entity pairs in abstracts. They utilized statistically significant relation pairs from the CTD database as one of the signal features to augment the confidence value for such feature sets. They achieved a high recall of 81.03% and averaged about 52.77% on F_1-score. Pons et al. (2015) employed the graph database (BRAIN) to screen out candidate relation pairs which were directly or indirectly associated with each other.

Le et al. (2015) and Li et al. (2015) both used SVM for classification based on various sets of lexical features. In one of the recent attempts on this task, Gu et al. (2017) applied a hybrid CNN and ME based model to handle multi and single sentence level relation pairs to acquire a performance of 61.30%. Although their model did not involve any KB-based refining, but post-processing strategies for filtering the relation pairs were employed. Our approach is also a ML dedicated approach in which the extracted patterns were used to develop SVM features based on the convolution tree kernel for learning. In contrast to all of the other methods, our approach achieved the highest recall rate of 85.08%, signifying that the features generated by our Invariance approach can identify positive association pairs with a higher specificity. Our F_1-score averaged at 54.34%, which is an overall satisfactory score but still falls short against the better systems based on KB and NN. The gap in performance can be overcome by improving the precision through additional resources to normalize the negative features. Holistically, our method as a feature-engineering tool is concise, more precise and feature flexible in comparison to other metrics used for feature generation. It can accommodate multiple features to adjust the size of polynomial and reduce the complexity in the evaluation of classifiers to make them more feasible, including simpler linear classifiers as well. The flexibility and power of this approach makes it an efficient choice for implementation with any learning algorithm.

Method	Precision	Recall	F_1-score
Li et al.	54.46	33.21	41.26
Le et al.	53.41	49.91	51.60
Alam et al.	39.12	81.03	52.77
Pons et al.	51.30	53.90	52.60
Xu et al.	55.67	58.44	57.03
Gu et al.	**55.70**	68.10	**61.30**
Our method	39.92	**85.08**	54.34

Table 2: Comparative Assessment of the CID task

5 Conclusion

This paper describes a novel method of feature engineering based on algebraic invariance, which in conjunction with SVM tree kernel-based approach is effective in identifying relation pairs for the CID task. Comparative analysis demonstrates that the method is powerful enough to identify diverse patterns/features within any corpus set without auxiliary resources. Therefore, we conjecture that our method as a feature generation tool can be highly effective and easily adoptable in various application scenarios.

For further enhancement in the future, we plan to use deep learning methods for model development in conjunction with our approach to gauge the variability introduced by the various learning models in context of our method. Furthermore, we also plan to enlist context-specific knowledge bases to optimize our feature sets and improve the overall performance.

Acknowledgments

We are grateful for the constructive comments from three anonymous reviewers. This work was supported by grant MOST106-3114-E-001- 002 and MOST105-2221-E-001-008-MY3 from the Ministry of Science and Technology, Taiwan.

Reference

Danqi Chen and Christopher D Manning. 2014. A Fast and Accurate Dependency Parser using Neural Networks. *Proceedings of EMNLP 2014*

Leonard Eugene Dickson. 1914. Mathematical Monongraphs Algebraic Invariants, No.14. *John Wiley*, New York.

Daniel Keren. 1994. Using Symbolic Computation to Find Algebraic Invariants. *IEEE Transactions on Pattern Analysis and Machine Intelligence, Vol. 16, No 11*, Nov 1994.

Jinghang Gu, Longhua Qian, Guodong Zhou. 2015. Chemical-induced Disease Relation Extraction with Lexical Features. *Proceeding of the fifth BioCreative challenge evaluation workshop*, 2015

Jinghang Gu, Fuqing Sun, Longhua Qian, and Guodong Zhou. 2016. Chemical-induced disease relation extraction via convolutional neural network. *Database (2017)* Vol. 2017

Leaman R, Wei C-H, Lu Z. tmChem: a high performance approach for chemical named entity recognition and normalization. *Journal of Cheminformatics*. 2015;7(Suppl 1):S3. doi:10.1186/1758-2946-7-S1-S3.

Robert Leaman, Rezarta Islamaj Doğan, Zhiyong Lu; DNorm: disease name normalization with pairwise learning to rank, *Bioinformatics*, Volume 29, Issue 22, 15 November 2013, Pages 2909–2917

S. Kulick, A. Bies, M. Liberman, M. Mandel, R. McDonald, M. Palmer, A. Schein and L. Ungar. 2004. Integrated Annotation for Biomedical Information Extraction, *HLT/NAACL 2004 Workshop: Biolink 2004, pp. 61-68.*

Jiao Li, Yueping Sun, Robin J. Johnson, Daniela Sciaky, Chih-Hsuan Wei, Robert Leaman, Allan Peter Davis, Carolyn J.Mattingly, Thomas C. Wiegers, Zhiyong Lu. 2015. Annotating chemicals, diseases and their interactions in biomedical literature. *Proceedings of the fifth BioCreative challenge evaluation workshop*, 2015.

Alessandro Moschitti. 2006, Efficient Convolution Kernels for Dependency and Constituent Syntactic Trees. *Proceedings of the 17th European Conference on Machine Learning, Berlin, Germany, 2006.*

Alessandro Moschitti. 2004. A study on Convolution Kernels for Shallow Semantic Parsing. *Proceedings of the 42-th Conference on Association for Computational Linguistic (ACL-2004), Barcelona, Spain, 2004.*

E. Pons, B.F.H. Becker, S.A. Akhondi, Z. Afzal, E.M. van Mulligen, J.A. Kors. 2015. RELigator: Chemical-disease relation extraction using prior knowledge and textual information. *Proceeding of the fifth BioCreative challenge evaluation workshop*, 2015

Richard Socher, John Bauer, Christopher D. Manning and Andrew Y. Ng. 2013. Parsing With Compositional Vector Grammars. *Proceedings of ACL 2013*

Yoshimasa Tsuruka, Yuka Tateishi, Jin-Dong Kim, Tomoko Ohta, John McNaught, Sophia Ananiadou, and Jun'ichi Tsujii. 2005. Developing a Robust Part-of-Speech Tagger for Biomedical Text, *Advances in Informatics - 10th Panhellenic Conference on Informatics, LNCS 3746, pp. 382-392, 2005*

Yoshimasa Tsuruoka and Jun'ichi Tsujii. 2005. Bidirectional Inference with the Easiest-First Strategy for Tagging Sequence Data, *Proceedings of HLT/EMNLP 2005, pp. 467-474*

Chih-Hsuan Wei, Yifan Peng, Robert Leaman, Allan Peter Davis, Carolyn J. Mattingly, Jiao Li Thomas C. Wiegers and Zhiyong Lu. 2015. Assessing the state of the art in biomedical relation extraction: overview of the BioCreative V chemical-disease relation (CDR) task. *Database,* 2015.

Jun Xu, Yonghui Wu, Yaoyun Zhang, Jingqi Wang, Ruiling Liu, Qiang Wei, and Hua Xu. 2015. UTH-CCB@BioCreative V CDR Task: Identifying Chemical-induced Disease Relations in Biomedical Text . *Proceeding of the fifth BioCreative challenge evaluation workshop*, 2015

Huiwei Zhou, Huijie Deng, Jiao He. 2015. Chemical-disease Relations Extraction Based on The Shortest Dependency Path Tree. *Proceeding of the fifth BioCreative challenge evaluation workshop*, 2015

Author Index

Abd Yusof, Noor Fazilla, 9
Adam, Dillon C, 39
Almeida, Luan, 39
Aramaki, Eiji, 18

Badman, Steven, 39
Batongbacal, Sean, 39

Chang, Yi-Chun, 26
Chang, Yung-Chun, 26, 57
Chughtai, Abrar, 39

Dai, Hong-Jie, 26, 33

Fu, Tzu-Yuan, 26

Guerin, Frank, 9

Han-Chen, Daniel, 39
Hsu, Wen-Lian, 26, 57
Huang, Yi-Jie, 26

ISO, Hayate, 18
Ito, Kaoru, 18

Jonnagaddala, Jitendra, 26, 39

Kerren, Andreas, 1
Kim, Juae, 47
Ko, Youngjoong, 47
Kwon, Sunjae, 47

Lai, Po-Ting, 52
Lin, Chenghua, 9

MacIntyre, C Raina, 39
Mundekkat, Jumail M, 39

Seo, Jungyun, 47
Singh, Onkar, 33
Skeppstedt, Maria, 1
Stede, Manfred, 1
Su, Chu Hsien, 26

Takeuchi, Ryo, 18
Tang, Zhao-Li, 33
Ting, Tseng-Hsin, 26
Tsai, Richard Tzong-Han, 52
Tu, Jing Cyun, 52

Wakamiya, Shoko, 18
Wang, Chen-Kai, 33
Wang, Rou-Min, 26
Warikoo, Neha, 57

Yang, Jenny J, 39

Zhu, Jing Z, 39

Association for Computational Linguistics
209 N. Eighth Street
Stroudsburg, Pennsylvania 18360

ISBN 978-1-5108-5299-0

CURRAN ASSOCIATES INC.
proceedings
.com